THE AMERICAN REVOLUTION

America's successful breakaway from Britain was one of the most crucial landmarks of modern times. Yet it did not start with a single unanimous decision by the Thirteen Colonies, but rather with a quickening, unpremeditated drift into rebellion and war.

Drawing on hundreds of contemporary illustrations, this addition to the WAYLAND PICTORIAL SOURCES SERIES portrays the background to the crisis, the drawing together of the Colonies, the creation of an American army, and the tactics and strategies adopted by Congress, George Washington, and the other generals to win independence from the sovereignty of George III. The author studies the divisions in Colonial policies and loyalties that threw up a barrier against any cohesive national spirit; he shows, how, when the war began, the Colonists seemed ill-equipped to defy Britain's greater military strength; how the new-born states had to bury their differences in common cause, and from the frontiersmen and militiamen create an effective force which could be fielded against the experienced British redcoats.

Here is a graphic study of how the Colonists organized their fight for freedom, and deflated British over-confidence. All the major campaigns and engagements are examined, from the opening of hostilities at Lexington and Concord, the siege of Boston, the British capture of Philadelphia, through the ebb and flow of the struggle to the historic surrender of Cornwallis at Yorktown. In the final sections the author makes an assessment of the years following Britain's withdrawal, in which the new nation was left to deal with the devastation of war, and the pressing problems of peace.

THE WAYLAND PICTORIAL SOURCES SERIES

THE AMERICAN REVOLUTION

ROGER PARKINSON

WAYLAND PUBLISHERS LONDON

The Wayland Pictorial Sources Series

Frontispiece: The Death of General Mercer at the Battle of Princeton (3rd January, 1777)

Picture research by the Publishers

Copyright © 1971 by Wayland (Publishers) Ltd
101 Grays Inn Road London WC1

SBN 85340 027 x

Printed by Jarrold and Sons Ltd, Norwich

CONTENTS

TABLE OF DATES

1763 *February 10th* Treaty of Paris
October 7th Proclamation of 1763
1764 *April 5th* Sugar Act
April 19th Currency Act
1765 *March 22nd* Stamp Act
October 7th Stamp Act Congress
opens
1766 *March 18th* Repeal of Stamp Act
March 18th Declaratory Act
1767 *June 29th* Townshend Duties
1770 *March 5th* Boston Massacre
April 12th Townshend Duties lifted
except on tea
1773 *May 10th* Tea Act
December 16th Boston Tea Party
1774 *March 31st* Coercive Acts
September 5th First Continental Congress opens
1775 *April 19th* Lexington and Concord
May 10th Second Continental Congress opens
May 10th Rebel capture of Ticonderoga
June 15th Washington becomes Commander-in-Chief
June 17th Bunker Hill
1776 *January 10th* Paine's *Common Sense* appears
March 17th British evacuation of Boston
June 7th Lee's resolution for independence debated by Congress
July 2nd Resolution adopted
July 4th Declaration of Independence
August 17th Battle for Long Island
October 28th White Plains

November 16th Port Washington taken
December 26th Trenton
1777 *January 3rd* Princeton
July 6th Burgoyne re-takes Ticonderoga
August 6th Orkiskany
August 16th Bennington
September 11th Brandywine
September 19th Freeman's Farm
September 20th Paoli
September 26th British take Philadelphia
October 4th Germantown
October 7th Bemis Heights
October 17th Burgoyne surrenders at Saratoga
1778 *February 6th* Franco-American treaty
June 28th Monmouth
July 5th Clark takes Kaskaskia
November 11th Cherry Valley massacre
December 29th British take Savannah
1779 *February 25th* Clark takes Vincennes
July 16th Stony Point
August 19th Paulus Hook
September 16th Siege of Savannah starts
October 20th Savannah falls
1780 *May 12th* Charleston falls
June 23rd Springfield
August 16th Camden
October 7th King's Mountain
1781 *January 1st* Pennsylvania Line mutinies
January 17th Cowpens
March 15th Guilford Courthouse

April 25th Hobkirk's Hill
September 8th Eutaw Springs
September 28th Siege of Yorktown
   begins

October 19th Cornwallis surrenders
1783 *April 19th* Congress proclaims end of
   war
September 3rd Peace Treaty

CHAPTER ONE

THE SLIDE TO WAR

IN 1763, Britain seemed to stand at the peak of her power and prestige. She had defeated her nearest rival, France, and forced her to sign the humiliating Treaty of Paris. She ruled possessions throughout the known world—in India, Sumatra, the West Indies, Africa, the Mediterranean, Central America, Newfoundland and Canada. But the most thriving territory of all comprised the Thirteen Colonies in North America. In Britain, the birth of the Industrial Revolution was promising wealth and progress. The monarchy stood in firm control, both of the country and Parliament. The last serious internal threat to the Crown, posed by the Stuart claimant Bonnie Prince Charlie and his French-supported Catholic Jacobites, had been crushed on the bloody battlefield of Culloden in 1746.

Yet in twenty hectic years Britain was to be defeated by her own subjects, the faraway inhabitants of those Thirteen Colonies of North America. The great British Army which had routed the French in the Seven Years' War (1756–63) was to suffer humiliation at the hands of the Colonists at Yorktown. The redcoats would be forced to lay down their arms before an army of revolutionaries led by General George Washington.

The American War of Independence (1774–83) was to be fought in three main regions of the Colonies: north, south, and west. Each area was to have its own characteristics: the skirmishes and in-credible hardships in the forests and across the icy rivers of Quebec and New England; the manoeuvrings and campaigns of position in the heart of the Carolinas and Georgia; and the brutal operations by and against savage Indians, supported by the British in the long Ohio Valley. In each of these three arenas of war the Colonists would eventually win. Fourteen military actions would yield decisive results, in which the defeated force was either completely captured or destroyed. In nine of these, the British were to be the losers. The names of these battles are still glorified by the victors—Moore's Creek, Trenton, Bennington, Saratoga, Vincennes, Stony Point, King's Mountain, Cowpens, Yorktown.

Yet George Washington, who eventually led the Americans to victory, only won two of these nine engagements. Only once, at Yorktown, could he dictate his own terms of surrender, and even then he had to share the laurels with his French allies. His defeats outnumbered his successes. He was not a brilliant strategist or tactician. But if Washington had more defeats, his victories meant more. In a sense, he epitomized the whole re-volutionary idea by his ability to work in the most adverse and difficult conditions, and by his dignity, loyalty, courage and dogged determination.

The Colonists faced two fundamental difficulties, quite apart from greater British resources and military strength.

Before war began, they had to unify Colonies and men who differed in outlook, aims, temperament and allegiance to the idea of an independent American nation; and they had to preserve this unity during the hard years of struggle in order to win military victory. In the face of economic and social hardships (as well as military), they had to build and buttress some structure of government even in the midst of war. When victory and peace came, the struggle entered a third phase, a struggle to remain united when the armies had marched away. The threat of national collapse remained as strong, if not stronger, than before. Friction between state authority and central government power, which had long existed, grew even more painful. Against such a canvas, a permanent system of government, and the Constitution of the United States of America, had to be forged.

The outbreak of rebellion against Britain astonished most people as much as the result. In 1763 most Colonists were loyal to Britain and were content to live under the rule of the Crown. Yet within twelve years, fighting had begun. The reasons for this slide into war during those years are to be found on two levels. On the first were the more immediate obvious causes—typified and illustrated by events like the Boston Massacre and Boston Tea Party, stemming from economic and commercial "interference" on the part of London. But there was a deeper, more fundamental level. Far more important for the future, this involved issues of human rights and the dignity of mankind. Some Colonial leaders fought not only for their own freedom, but for the concept of freedom for all men. To set the American Revolution in its proper perspective, we must examine this underlying current, which flowed strongly throughout the 1760s and which carried the Thirteen Colonies downstream into the whirlpool of war.

While the Thirteen Colonies were far from unified in the 1760s, a common identity was gradually emerging. The terms "America" and "Americans" were gaining popular currency. The economy was sound, the government a stable one; Americans had little need of Britain. Inevitably, the relationship between Colonies and Mother Country would be questioned. This questioning was very much in the tradition of the Age of Enlightenment. Successive writers had expressed it by 1774, and their work helped to create a revolutionary doctrine. By challenging England's right to tax them without their own consent, the Colonists eventually came to challenge the right of anyone to govern men at all, against the wishes of the governed. The political philosophy of these American thinkers was based on and adapted from the teachings of writers in the Old World. The thoughts of John Locke, the English philosopher, seemed especially relevant (1). In his

1

Two Treatises of Government (1690), Locke had said that only political power used "for the public good" can be justified. Government is a trust, he wrote, forfeited by a ruler who fails to secure this public good. People always have the right to withdraw their support and overthrow the government if it fails to fulfil its trust. In France, the philosopher Jean-Jacques Rousseau developed similar ideas (2). Rousseau believed that sovereignty was the people's own birthright. The people delegated it to kings and governments through an implied social contract, but kept the right to take action if this trust was abused. This idea was developed by Denis Diderot (3). In his great *Encyclopedie* (1751) he added that a government's main concern must be for the common good of the people (4). These ideas, shared by the Marquis de Condorcet (5), Voltaire (6) and other French political thinkers in their philosophical debates (7), appealed to the American Colonial leaders.

2

ENCYCLOPÉDIE,
OU
DICTIONNAIRE RAISONNÉ
DES SCIENCES,
DES ARTS ET DES MÉTIERS.

5

3

4

6

7

A young American planter and lawyer, Thomas Jefferson was greatly influenced by the European "natural law" philosophers (8). Attracted at first to the writing of John Locke and Charles de Montesquieu (9), he turned to Richard Bland's *Enquiry into the Rights of the British Colonies* in which his fellow Virginian also asserted the natural rights of man. Jefferson declared in the Virginia House of Burgesses that, as the Colonists had been given life, liberty and property by their Creator, the British Government must protect that gift and not reduce it. He developed his views in *A Summary View of the Rights of British America*. Here, he appealed to King George III to pay attention to pleas made by the Colonists as "he is no more than the chief officer of the people, appointed by the laws, and circumscribed with definite powers." The British Colonies, Jefferson added, had been founded by free Britons using their natural right to create new societies under such laws as

8   9

seemed "most likely to promote public happiness." Colonists owed no more political allegiance to the people of Britain than did the British to surviving Angles and Saxons. Jefferson argued that the link with Britain was a contractual one; and the contract could be ended. Two years later, after hostilities had begun, the Declaration of Independence was issued by the Continental Congress (10). This stated that American Colonial rights had been violated, and announced that political bonds between the American State and Britain were broken. Jefferson himself took a major part in drafting the Declaration. The similarity with his *Summary View* is seen in this famous passage from the Declaration: "We hold these truths to be self-evident, that all men are created equal, that they are endowed by their Creator with certain unalienable Rights, that among these are Life, Liberty and the pursuit of Happiness."

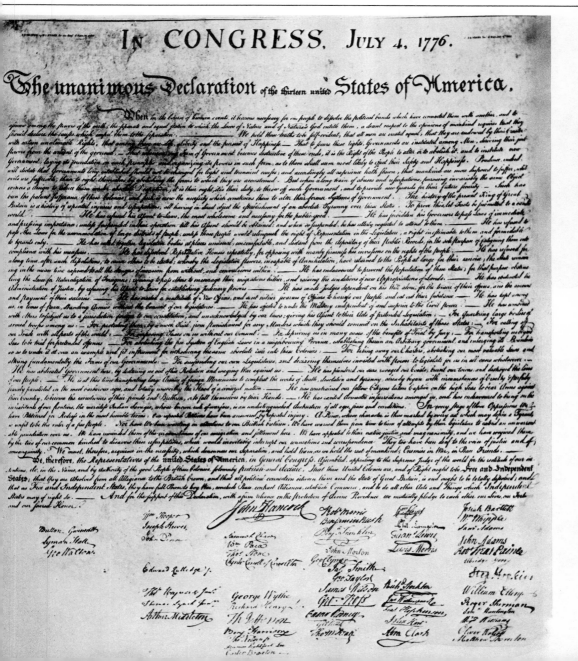

Another man played an important part in the drafting and issue of the Declaration of Independence, if more indirectly. This was an Englishman, Thomas Paine, who had settled in Pennsylvania in 1774 (11). In January, 1776, Paine's *Common Sense* made its sensational appearance (12). This pamphlet reflected ideas already proposed by men like John Adams (13) and Thomas Jefferson. It was written in superb propagandist style, in language overflowing with emotion. Many thousands of copies were printed and it reached an immense reading public. Once again, the "natural law" argument was stressed. The Patriots in America should become the champions not merely of liberty, but of the rights of mankind, wrote Paine. Government was at best "a necessary evil," but government by monarchy was worst of all, and George III was a deplorable King (14). The first King in most royal lines, he said, was "nothing better than the principal ruffian of

11

12

13

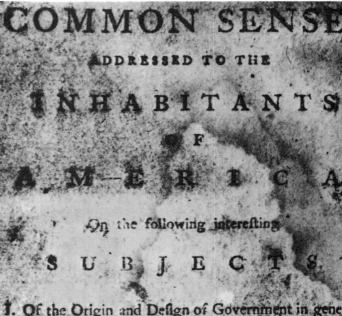

COMMON SENSE

ADDRESSED TO THE

INHABITANTS

OF

AMERICA

On the following interesting

SUBJECTS

I. Of the Origin and Design of Government in general with concise Remarks on the English Constitution.

II. Of Monarchy and Hereditary Succession.

III. Thoughts on the present State of American Affairs.

IV. Of the present Ability of America, with some miscellaneous Reflections.

Man knows no Master save creating HEAVEN,
Or those whom Choice and common Good ordain.
THOMSON

NEWPORT:

Printed and Sold by SOLOMON SOUTHWICK

M,DCC,LXXVI.

some restless gang." Kings won power for no better reason than that they had killed their enemies. Logically, the English people owed nothing to William of Normandy or to his heirs. Nor did the Americans owe anything to the English, Paine added. The time had come to draw apart. "O! Ye that love mankind! Ye that dare oppose not only tyranny but the tyrant, stand forth! Every spot of the old world is overrun with oppression. Freedom hath been hunted round the globe . . . O! receive the fugitive, and prepare in time an asylum for mankind." Some American politicians, including John Adams, disliked *Common Sense*. But Paine gave voice to the feelings which many Americans had and which they had not so far expressed. Patriots throughout the Thirteen Colonies came forward to demand that America stand alone; and in July of the year that *Common Sense* appeared, the Declaration of Independence was adopted.

14

But there were many in America who still hesitated, even at the time of the Declaration of Independence. Opposition to Britain grew slowly. As late as 1775, Benjamin Franklin (15) believed that, if Parliament stopped claiming the right to tax, trouble could be avoided; and at that time Jefferson still considered America's aim should be "dependence on Great Britain, properly limited." The resentment was directed at first against Parliament, and not the King himself. Thus the Declaration of Rights was sent direct to the King, together with a petition to him and an "Address to the People of Great Britain." Parliament was ignored. Even friendship for the British people did not die completely, nor did reverence for the British Crown. The philosophical talk of natural rights was restricted to a small although influential group, at least until *Common Sense* appeared. It did not

15   16   17

18

belong in the life of the settler (16), nor in the rich Colonist's drawing or dining rooms (17). Moreover, there was fear. A break with Britain meant a step into the unknown. If America was not a British possession, what would she be? So, before, and even during the war, there were conflicting ideas over America's aims. The Conservatives believed that when peace came there should be a return to the pre-war situation with themselves governing instead of the British. Radicals or Democrats, like Patrick Henry (18), wanted a more democratic system and far-reaching reforms, for example, universal adult suffrage. Liberals, including Jefferson and James Madison, were more moderate, standing between the other two main groups. Britain could have used American hesitation before the war to help come to an agreement. But her policies were too rigid.

Inevitably, the young King George III's reaction to talk of "natural rights" was one of horror (19). He had little time for anyone who, like the English radical John Wilkes, questioned his authority, English or American. The Colonists believed that their rights had been violated: George III believed that his leniency with the Colonists had been abused. The Americans had not kept in their place; they must be brought to heel. There could be no question of discussion. Voltaire had made Locke's philosophy fashionable in Europe: but not with George III. George looked with more approval on the burning of Rousseau's book *Du Contrat Social* at Geneva in 1763 (20). George's first minister and favourite, the Marquis of Bute (21), thought the same; and Parliament too was very much influenced by the King. But on the American issue no governing ministry wished to defy the King's wishes, in any case. Nothing must be given away, least of all on taxation. When the

19

21

20

22

Stamp Act of 1765 was repealed in 1766, a Declaratory Act at once reaffirmed Parliament's right to impose taxes just as it had done with the duties imposed by the 1765 Stamp Act. Both sides of the Atlantic clashed in a battle of words and high-sounding principles. In 1770 William Pitt (23) declared, even though he sympathized with the Colonists, that they "must be subordinate. In all laws relating to trade and navigation, this is the mother country, they are children. They must obey and we prescribe." Yet principles alone do not cause war, not even if proposed by "the man unique in all ages" as Voltaire was renowned in Paris in 1778 (22). Something more was needed to spark the fuse, namely the inflammable chain of events which came after 1763. This level of the origins of the war shows, even more clearly than the deep doctrinal difference between the two countries, the folly and blindness of Britain.

23

CHAPTER TWO

THE SEVENTEEN-SIXTIES

PROBABLY BRITAIN's greatest error was to misconstrue the Thirteen Colonies—their attitudes, capabilities and levels of society. Too few first hand reports reached London, and these were often biased or ignored. In 1778, when it was far too late, the English prime minister Lord North sent three envoys to hold discussions with the Americans. One, William Eden, complained in a letter to his brother that the British had ignorantly thrown away a great Empire. "It is impossible to give you any adequate idea of the vast scale of this country. I know little more of it than I saw in coming 150 miles up the Delaware, but I know enough to regret most heartily that our rulers instead of making the tour of Europe did not finish their education by a voyage round the coasts and rivers of the western side of the Atlantic." In another letter: "It is impossible to see even what I have seen of this magnificent country and not to go nearly mad at the long train of misconducts and mischances by which we have lost it." From British ignorance came the legislative mistakes in the years just before the outbreak of hostilities and which were the immediate causes of the war.

If the Colonists were nearer to nationhood than the British realized, it is wrong to dramatize Britain's mistake. Although the Colonists were acquiring a national identity, and calling themselves Americans, they were not a nation. Rather they thought of themselves as Virginians, Rhode Islanders, Jerseymen, North or South Carolinians. Each Colony had a separate government, under the authority of London. Communications between cities and Colonies were bad. Colony quarrelled with Colony: a 21-year long dispute over Fort Pitt embittered Virginia and Pennsylvania; Connecticut claimed parts of Wyoming Valley along the Susquehanna; New Hampshire and New York clashed over possession of the Green Mountains. Apart from these disputes, there were differences between North and South, East and West. Geographical divisions marked social and economic discords. Conflicts between East and West resulted in violence, with the inland territories—whose inhabitants were less educated and rougher than those on the coastal fringes—believing they were treated as second-class citizens. These settlers often lacked proper representation in the colonial assemblies. Easterners, not exposed to attack from Indians, were reluctant to pay for inland defence; in 1764 Pennsylvania frontiersmen marched against Philadelphia and the Quaker pacificists who thought it wrong to fight the Indians. Differences between North and South became one of the two great threats to unity in the war against Britain and in the subsequent peace. The South had a different economic and social structure to that of the North, as did the East and West. Aristocratic society was more firmly established in the South.

Rural influences were also stronger in the South. Of the five most densely populated areas only one (around Charleston) lay in the South. The Mason-Dixon line which set the boundary between Maryland and Pennsylvania was not drawn until 1767, but within twenty years it was recognized as separating two distinct parts of the continent. In all these ways America lacked cohesion. During the War of Independence, thirteen independent states fought in temporary alliance.

Nor was Britain completely united. Parliament and Crown might dismiss American talk of "natural law" and the "rights of man", but some Englishmen sympathized with the American view. One was Dr. Josiah Tucker, Dean of Gloucester, who wrote a tract *The True Interests of Great Britain Set Forth in Regard to the Colonies*. Tucker felt that the Colonists could not be held in subjection for ever. Indeed, he thought that all subjects overseas would one day win independence. This applied to French and Spanish colonies too, but the Americans were moving faster because they already had more freedom. Even if they were subdued for a while by force, this would only increase their hatred of Britain, and their demands for independence. Tucker advised Britain to liberate the Thirteen Colonies of her own will, before being compelled to do so. Support for America also came from English Republicans and Radicals. The Radicals demanded far-reaching reforms in Parliament and denounced George III for manipulating elections. They also demanded freedom of the press.

The leading figure in the radical movement was John Wilkes, author of many scandalous pamphlets, hero of the restless London mobs, and a stirring advocate of Colonial aims. More powerful opponents of George III and his minister, Lord North, were the Marquis of Rockingham, William Pitt (Earl of Chatham) and their followers, the Chathamites. More moderate than Wilkes and the Radicals, the Rockingham Party opposed fundamental changes in the British political system. The Whigs in this faction chiefly wished to regain political power in London: they wanted to conciliate the Colonists not only on principle, but because the King and Lord North preferred force.

The Chathamites too wanted power and personal position. But Lord Chatham himself wished to preserve the Empire intact. This was largely why he spoke up for the Colonists; he wanted a peaceful settlement short of American independence. Yet he was still a thorn in the Government's side. On 19th January, 1775, he praised the people of Massachusetts for defending their rights, and said how much he admired the First Continental Congress. Chatham was to consult Benjamin Franklin and was prepared to do much to meet Congressional demands. But by then it was too late.

But if Britain also lacked unanimity, her discords were not as great as those of the Colonists. George III and his ministries had firm control; John Wilkes and his fellow Radicals commanded very few votes in the House of Commons; Chatham delayed too long; and in the earlier years he too had given his assent to Townshend and the Stamp Act. Time was running out, and human mistakes were exacerbating the basic doctrinal differences.

On 10th February, 1763, when the Treaty of Paris ended the Seven Years' War, King Louis XV of France (24) ceded to Britain all Canada and all that part of Louisiana (except for New Orleans) lying east of the Mississippi. Spain yielded Florida. All the eastern third of North America came under British control (25). Britain, according to hostile cartoons, had carved up the world (26). But Britain still had to pay the price of war. The national debt exceeded £130 million; taxes had soared and taxpayers shouted for them to be cut. Bute's ministry had to find money from elsewhere. Why not from America? On 23rd February, Welbore Ellis, Secretary at War, announced that the British army based in North America was "to be supported the first year by England, afterwards by the Colonies." Partly due to a feeling that some of the Colonies had helped too little in the war, there was mount-

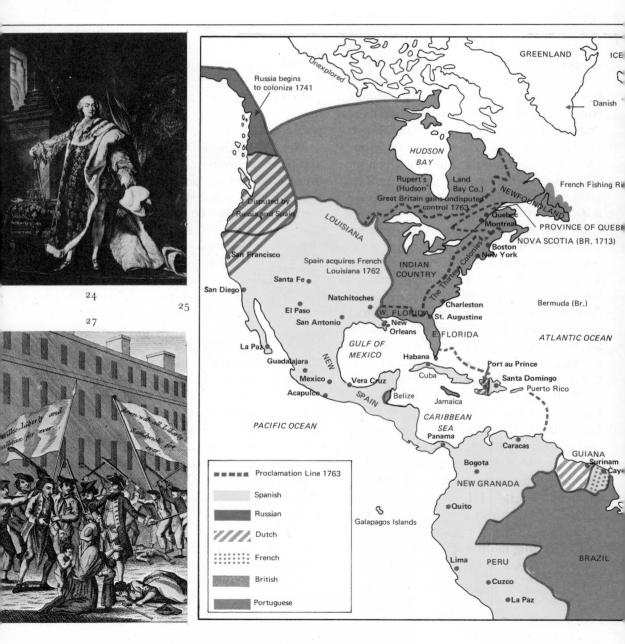

24

25

27

Proclamation Line 1763

Spanish

Russian

Dutch

French

British

Portuguese

ing pressure upon America to pay more now. In April, 1763, the Earl of Bute retired as prime minister, but plans to make the Colonies contribute to the support of the British Army advanced under his successor, George Grenville. But a delay followed: Grenville became involved in a clash with John Wilkes. That troublesome journalist condemned the Grenvillites as tools of Bute, and George III as an enemy of British liberties. His scurrilous writings stirred up unrest (27), and Wilkes fled to France in December to escape arrest. A major opponent of the official line now made his entrance—Edmund Burke, who was elected a Member of Parliament in 1765 (28). His speeches against the Stamp Act lifted him to fame and his oratory in 1774 and 1775 helped to support liberal imperialism. But in 1770 Lord North (29) became prime minister; he was an obedient instrument for George III.

26

28

29

Much was wrong with Britain's political and administrative machine. Members of Parliament were responsible to the monarch, George III, not yet twenty-five years old. The House of Commons itself was undemocratic, based on unequal electoral districts. The electoral system was often abused by so-called "election dinners" to win votes (30) and on the actual polling day (31). There was no coherent party organization in England. The Whigs (including merchants, religious dissenters, radicals)

had fallen apart into factions, the largest of which was led by the aged Duke of Newcastle (32), and another by William Pitt (33). The King made full use of royal patronage, forming a group of supporters known as the "King's Friends"; he was able to make his former tutor, the Earl of Bute, First Lord of the Treasury (equivalent to prime minister today), keeping him in office until the Spring of 1763. Thereafter, the political situation became even more fluid and unstable. George III was

30

31

unable to find a ministerial grouping that pleased him until Lord North took office in 1770. Instability at the top of the administration was reflected by weakness lower down. In 1768 the post of Secretary for American Affairs was created, with Lord Hillsborough being appointed to it. But neither Lord Hillsborough nor Lord Dartmouth, who took over in 1772, were qualified for the post. No single agency in London was fully responsible for the Colonies, and proper consultation was made even more unlikely. Nor, if laws were passed, were they fully enforced. Tax laws reaped more bitterness than revenue. Customs officers were lax: in America they collected no more than £2,000 ($10,000) in duties each year, although tax administration cost up to £8,000 ($40,000) a year. In London, the mob often virtually ruled (34), and law enforcement was handled by the local military (35). If authority at home was clumsy, crude (36), or powerless, then how much more so was it in America.

32

35

33

34

36

A major trans-Atlantic bond was forged by trading. The Thirteen Colonies produced more food than they could eat, so grain and flour were exported from the Middle Colonies, and rice from South Carolina and Georgia (37). Virginia and Maryland sent tobacco to Britain (38). Furs and skins were loaded into trading vessels at many Colonial ports. But if foreign markets were profitable, they were not essential. For Britain, trade was a different matter, and had to be vigorously protected, as by the Navigation Acts of 1651, 1660 and 1696 which confined the carrying trade within the Empire to British or Colonial vessels. These Acts also banned certain goods from being shipped abroad. Britain worked to retain a tight grip on Colonial trade, and tried to ensure that only British goods were bought in America. Wharfs at ports such as Bristol (39) and London had to be kept fully employed. The Bank of England (40), Mansion House (Lord Mayor of London's residence) and

37

38

39

40

41

Royal Exchange (41) remained the well-protected pillars of Empire. So, too, did companies like the South Sea Company and the East India Company (42). As a result, a source of conflict with the growing American Colonies was ever-present; even if the Navigation Acts fostered Colonial as well as British merchant shipping industries (over a third of the vessels carrying the British flag were built in American shipyards). This irritation was vented upon customs offices (43) and other symbols of British colonial administration. And as in other areas, the sources of conflict were aggravated by lack of local knowledge, especially on the part of London officials and politicians. Communications were difficult with America; up to twenty weeks were consumed in despatching messages and receiving replies. Edmund Burke observed, "Seas roll and months pass between order and execution (44)."

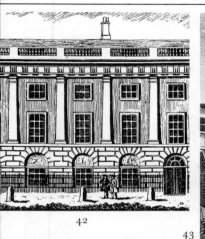

42

43

44

A gulf of misunderstanding, as wide as the Atlantic, was always ready to open up. Yet the Colonists had much to be pleased with, even under British rule. Each of the Thirteen Colonies had its own Parliament, called the House of Burgesses in Virginia (45), the Commons House, House of Delegates and House of Commons elsewhere. These bodies, all of them elected, had little control over external or maritime affairs, but they did retain a strong grip on internal matters. Nor did London exert a strong, autocratic interference. Two of the Colonies, Connecticut and Rhode Island, were virtually autonomous. In Pennsylvania, the charter given to William Penn (46) meant that the governor, chosen by the Penns, could personally veto laws. Governors posted from London came and went, but the assemblies continued, gaining rather than losing strength. Some royal governors, judges and officials, even depended upon the elected Colonial bodies for their

45

46

salaries. Royal control was sometimes felt to be less onerous than that of American proprietors in the Colonies, with their powerful seals of authority (47, 48). In 1765 Benjamin Franklin was even sent (vainly) to England to ask that Penn's proprietorship be abolished and that George III assume direct control. Men who worked in the Colonial assemblies were often brilliant in the art of government. Many of their voices were soon to be heard across the Atlantic. They included John Adams, a Harvard graduate and rising lawyer; his cousin Samuel Adams (49), more reactionary, and a powerful propagandist; Benjamin Franklin who had worked as a journeyman printer (50), producing among other items bank notes (51), and who was an effective agent for Georgia, New Jersey, Massachusetts and Pennsylvania in London; Thomas Jefferson, who was first elected to the House of Burgesses in 1769 when only twenty-six years old and the Virginian lawyer, Patrick Henry.

49

47

48

50

51

These men, and others like them, were often ignored by the London politicians. One main reason for this was lack of real appreciation of Colonial life. Londoners forgot, or did not know, that America also had her wealthy landowners and her rich urban dwellers, dressed in the finest European fashions (52), and living in their elegant mansions (53) surrounded by all the comforts of eighteenth-century life; their chairs and sideboards made by fine Colonial craftsmen (54), their carpets and fabrics imported from India. On the tobacco and cotton plantations and in Philadelphia, Boston, New York, Charleston and Newport, the American social hierarchy prospered. The citizens were far removed from the "uncouth Colonials" that many Englishmen imagined. Colleges were being founded: Harvard College, Cambridge, Massachusetts (55) in 1638, and King's College (56) (later Columbia University), New York City in 1754. So were museums and libraries. The

52

53   54

social structure did, however, differ from that in England, Germany, Spain and France. Class distinctions were less sharply drawn. The population sprang from varied origins; for example, about one third of the people of Pennsylvania were German, and continued read newspapers in their own language (57). In addition, one in every five Americans was of African descent. Slaves still arrived each year in America, packed into the holds of slave-ships (58). The slave system, mainstay of the southern plantations, endured for many years; but already there was pressure to restrict it. This pressure was to grow rapidly. George Washington, Thomas Jefferson, Patrick Henry, Alexander Hamilton, John Adams, John Jay, James Madison, all of them, Northerners and Southerners alike, were to condemn slavery. Indeed, the slave system gave ammunition to the British: "How can the Colonists talk of freedom when they themselves are slave-owners?"

55

56   57

◄(No. I)►

Philadelphische Zeitung.

SAMBSTAG, den 6 Mey. 1732.

58

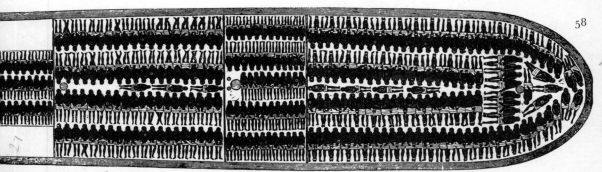

Apart from the wealthy hierarchy, three main levels of population were to be found in the Colonies. These included a surprisingly high percentage of middle-class urban dwellers. The largest of the cities, Philadelphia, Boston and New York, were comparable in size to Leeds, Sheffield and Bristol in England at that time, and many towns counted over 2,000 inhabitants. Perhaps one in every twenty families lived for the most part in clapboard houses. Together with some houses built of brick and stone, these had long replaced the huts and log cabins of the early coastal settlers (60). Franklin and Washington sprang from this level of society, and their birthplaces were typical. Picture (61) shows Franklin's birthplace in Boston, and (62) shows Washington's in Westmoreland County, Virginia. The largest social group were the farmers, living in the woods of New England (59), the lush lowlands of the Hudson River (63), and the wilderness of Pennsylvania (64). The

population as a whole was expanding rapidly, doubling every generation: two million in 1763, two and a half million by 1775, and just under four million by 1790. Thousands of settlers continued to arrive at ports like Savannah (65). The average number of children in Colonial families was 7.5. Franklin reckoned that within a century the Colonies would have a greater population than Britain. In these circumstances, the Colonists wanted to push westward, not to find more space—

there was still plenty left in the East—but to farm new lands. Here, then, was the third stratum of society: the frontiersmen. Into the fringe areas of the Blue Ridge Mountains came the young George Washington as a surveyor (66), meeting the settlers, Indians and trappers. Here in these border regions the harshest and most primitive conditions were to be found, conditions which most London politicians wrongly believed were typical of the Thirteen Colonies.

60

61

62

59

64

63

65

66

As the Colonists pushed westward, they inevitably clashed with the native Indians. Skirmishes, ambushes (67), and massacres (68) were endless. Men lived, worked, and even worshipped in church, with guns close at hand (69). The British had tried to use the Indians during the Seven Years' War, but the Indians played French and British off against one another. In 1755 a combined French and Redskin force heavily defeated a British force under Major-General Edward Braddock (70) and, when the French withdrew, the Indians took to fighting the British in 1763. Fighting continued sporadically until late 1765. Because of the Indian fighting and the war with the French, British garrisons were left scattered throughout the frontier regions; and when the Seven Years' War was over, British politicians believed that the Colonists should pay toward the cost. The Colonists objected strongly. At the same time, the British tried to regulate the flow of emigrants to the West. A

67

68   69

70

71

Royal Proclamation of 7th October, 1763, created three new Colonies in North America: Quebec, and East and West Florida. But it also closed the land between the Appalachian Mountains and the Mississippi to occupation by white men. The Proclamation was an irritant, but did not stop expansion. "Long Hunters" led by Daniel Boone (71) moved deep into Kentucky; the Ohio Valley was settled by Virginians; Virginians and North Carolinians settled in the Tennessee Valley; and South Carolinians and Georgians moved towards the ridges of the southern Appalachians. Treaties (74) and trading (72, 73) were used to acquire land peacefully, but these means often failed. Clashes occurred between the settlers as well as with the Indians. There was bitter rivalry between men from New Hampshire and men from New York over the valuable territory of Vermont (75), and, ironically, New York vainly asked for help from British troops in 1773 and 1774.

72

73

74

75

CHAPTER THREE

THE END OF COMPROMISE

AGAINST A BACKGROUND of American growth, faulty British assessments, revival of British interest in the Colonies after 1763, the deficiencies of the London Parliament, poor communications and the stresses and strains of Colonial expansion, a series of events took place which flung Britain and America headlong into war. These events followed a cycle of legislation and reaction. This cycle widened the gap between Britain and the Thirteen Colonies; time and again the two sides clashed over the right of Parliament to tax, and the Colonists' right to be represented or consulted before taxes were levied. At times the gap might have been bridged, but these chances became less as time passed, and opportunities were overlooked until too late. When Britain did something to meet Colonial requests, as in 1770, only half-measures were taken and only a temporary political respite secured.

In the years 1763–74, Parliament had a succession of Governments; in his first decade as King, George III had no less than six ministries. The rapid changes caused confusion in policy, and the civil service failed to provide continuity of administration and advice while Governments came and went. With the inept policies and legislation of British leaders like Lord Bute, Lord Grenville, Lord Rockingham, Lord Grafton, Lord Townshend and ultimately Lord North, the relationship with America gradually moved nearer to disaster.

The first of these men, the Marquis of Bute, was a hollow character lacking in statesmanship. He awarded offices to fellow-Scotsmen and was accused of expanding the power of the King at Parliament's expense. Bute retired in April, 1763, unable to bear criticism from his fellow Members of Parliament: he was replaced by Lord George Grenville. Grenville only held power from spring 1763 to summer 1765. But during that short disastrous time, he implemented the decisions of the Bute ministry: a large force of British troops was to be garrisoned in North America, and the Colonies were to help pay for it. Taxes were now to be imposed on the Colonists, to relieve British taxpayers, and the Colonists were to provide billets and supplies for the troops. Grenville's ministry also tried to limit American westward expansion, partly by giving greater control over Indian affairs to British officials. It also tried to restrict American maritime trade and hampered the issue of American paper currency.

Grenville lost one of the last chances of averting a serious clash with the Thirteen Colonies when he refused to allow the Colonists a substitute for the stamp duties in February, 1765. After that, he gave place to the Marquis of Rockingham. Rockingham was more moderate toward the Colonists, but Townshend, his Chancellor of the Exchequer, aggravated the situation, and Lord North, his successor at the Exchequer and from 1770 the prime minister, was largely responsible for the final break.

Incompetence and lack of vision characterized those tragic years; attitudes steadily hardened. During the troubles of 1767–70 hundreds of thousands of Americans were turned against their mother country. American blood was to be shed, Americans killed in an event significantly titled a "massacre" even though the death toll was only six. Feelings by then were so influenced that the title was accepted and believed—so heightening the tension further.

Whitehall policies constituted a series of irritations. No British decision, by itself, was a great hardship for the Colonists. The Colonists would have purchased goods from British merchants without being ordered to; they would have sold raw materials to the British without being compelled; the Navigation Acts (tying Colonial trade to British ships) helped them as well as the British; and they could afford to pay the taxes. After the Stamp Act (1765) Benjamin Franklin advised friends in Philadelphia to save money so that they could pay the duties without trouble.

It is true that Virginian and Maryland tobacco planters were heavily penalized by having to send all their produce to foreign markets via England, where middlemen reaped rich profits. But these same planters did enjoy a monopoly. After all, Englishmen could not grow tobacco, nor was any but American tobacco allowed into Britain. While Britain preferred her own economic interests to those in America, she also preferred Colonial interests to those of foreigners. Men like John Adams and George Washington drank tea without wondering whether it had been taxed by Britain or had come from elsewhere. And yet the effects of these many pinpricks mounted. Each time legislation was passed, each time Whitehall mishandled the situation, indignation grew. Above all, as Franklin acidly noted in 1767, "Every man in England seems to consider himself as a piece of sovereign over America . . . and talks of *our subjects* in the Colonies."

Merchants and citizens were offended by the duties; planters and industrialists by trade restrictions; and even the frontiersman by such measures as the Quebec Act (1774), which pushed the boundaries of the province of Quebec southwest to the Ohio and Mississippi Rivers. This Act illustrates how far relations had deteriorated. In itself it was a reasonable and tolerant measure, creating some government over the area, where inadequate military supervision had existed before. But the Quebec Act was still viewed with suspicion by the Colonists. It was extremely ill-timed. Coming after the Boston Tea Party, although designed before news of this reached London, it was seen as a punitive measure; here was more British interference. When American supporters like Lord Chatham and Edmund Burke spoke out against it, the Colonists believed their suspicions were indeed well founded. Events by now had proceeded so far that the Colonists and British would believe almost anything about the other: provided it was critical.

When the war with France ended in 1763, the Prime Minister, Bute, wanted to maintain seventy-five infantry regiments in the British Army, and his successor, Grenville, decided that seventeen of them, about 8,500 men, should be stationed in North America. The Colonists' answer was to encourage desertion. In reply the British General, Thomas Gage, persuaded Parliament to revise the Mutiny Act, making the Colonists provide quarters and supplies. The soldiers were hated and jeered (76). However, Grenville was determined that the Colonists should pay toward the upkeep of the British Army in America, and in March, 1764, the American Act was passed. Duties on port and wine were raised, and a British judge was now appointed to sit in Halifax without a jury to try those accused of violating the maritime laws. At the same time, the Currency Act limited the issue of Colonial paper money (77). Then, in the spring of 1765, Grenville introduced a Stamp

76

78

79

77

Bill to raise up to £100,000 ($500,000) a year from the Colonists. Newspapers were taxed as were legal papers, commercial documents, pamphlets, playing cards and dice. The new law was to be effective from 1st November, 1765. In May, 1765, Patrick Henry condemned the proposed Act in a brilliant speech in the Virginia House of Burgesses, ending: "as for me, give me liberty or give me death!" (78). Other Colonial assemblies followed suit (79). Most Americans refused to buy the stamps (80, 81), which were often burned (82); troops escorting papers bearing the stamps were attacked (83). Incredibly, this reaction greatly astonished Parliament. But London opinion was now changing. Both Rockingham (the prime minister) and William Pitt felt that the Colonists should be consulted on taxation. On 22nd February, 1766, the Stamp Act was repealed amid universal joy in America (84), where cartoons depicted the "funeral of the Act" (85).

80

81

82

83

84 85

But the British would not give way completely. The customs system had been strengthened in 1764, and officials were now exacting full duties. More American ships suspected of smuggling were impounded than ever before (86) and, although the Stamp Act was repealed, a Declaratory Act re-affirmed Parliament's right to tax North America. Charles Townshend, as Chancellor of the Exchequer, irreparably damaged relations between London and America when, in May, 1766, he proposed duties on tea, glass, lead, paints and paper entering American ports. He wished to create a Board of Customs Commissioners in America to ensure regular payment of the duties. As these were external duties, Townshend felt that criticisms about the domestic taxation of the Stamp Act would be answered. The proposals became law in early summer, 1767. Soon after, Townshend died, to be replaced by the equally inept Lord North (87). In view of American opposition to the

86

87

88

The true Sons of Liberty

And Supporters of the Non-Importation Agreement,

ARE determined to refent any the leaft Infult or Menace offer'd to any one or more of the feveral Committees appointed by the Body at Faneuil-Hall, and chaftife any one or more of them as they deferve ; and will also fupport the Printers in any Thing the Committees fhall defire them to print.

AS a Warning to any one that fhall affront as aforefaid, upon fure Information given, one of thefe Advertifements will be pofted up at the Door or Dwelling-Houfe of the Offender.

duties, garrisons in the Middle Colonies were reinforced. During 1768 and 1769 the Colonies organized committees to boycott British goods, and warnings were given out to those importing goods into the country (88, 89, 90). Boston, the seat of the Board of Customs Commissioners, became a cauldron of discontent. Two more British regiments arrived there aboard a naval squadron late in 1768 (91). The tension continued to rise. In January, 1770, soldiers and civilians clashed during a riot, the "Battle of Golden Hill," but without casualties. In February a boy was killed when Ebenezer Richardson, a customs informer, fired on a threatening mob. On 5th March a sentry outside the Kings Street customs house was mobbed. Seven soldiers were hurriedly posted to the scene and in view of the intense provocation their officer, Captain Preston, gave the order to fire. Half a dozen civilians were slain in what quickly became known as the "Boston Massacre."

A LIST of the Names of those who AUDACIOUSLY continue to counteract the UNITED SENTIMENTS of the BODY of Merchants thro'out NORTH-AMERICA; by importing British Goods contrary to the Agreement.

John Bernard,
(In King-Street, almost opposite Vernon's Head.
James McMasters,
(On Treat's Wharf.
Patrick McMasters,
(Opposite the Sign of the Lamb.
John Mein,
(Opposite the White-Horse, and in King-Street.
Nathaniel Rogers,
(Opposite Mr. Henderson Inches Store lower End King-Street.
William Jackson,
At the Brazen Head, Cornhill, near the Town-House.
Theophilus Lillie,
(Near Mr. Pemberton's Meeting-House, North-End.
John Taylor,
(Nearly opposite the Heart and Crown in Cornhill.
Ame & Elizabeth Cummings,
(Opposite the Old Brick Meeting House, all of Boston.
Israel Williams, Esq; & Son,
(Traders in the Town of Hatfield.
And, Henry Barnes,
(Trader in the Town of Marlboro'.

89

WILLIAM JACKSON,

an IMPORTER; at the

BRAZEN HEAD,

North Side of the TOWN-HOUSE,

and Opposite the Town-Pump, in

Corn-hill, BOSTON.

It is desired that the SONS and DAUGHTERS of LIBERTY, would not buy any one thing of him, for in so doing they will bring Disgrace upon themselves, and their Posterity, for ever and ever, AMEN

90

VIEW OF PART OF THE TOWN OF BOSTON IN NEW ENGLAND AND BRITISH SHIPS OF WAR LANDING THEIR TROOPS! 1768

On the day of the Boston Massacre (92), Lord North's new ministry announced withdrawal of the duties, promising that there would be no new taxes. But, to save face, the duty on tea remained. Suspected British sympathizers were still "tarred and feathered" by Colonists (93). Yet in April, 1772, General Gage reported that America was in "profound tranquillity." He was much mistaken. Four weeks later the Royal Naval vessel *Gaspée* ran aground near Providence while chasing a suspected American smuggler. Rhode Islanders burned the ship (94) and wounded Dudlingston, the captain. In June next year the Massachusetts House of Representatives published letters written by their pro-British Governor, Thomas Hutchinson, revealing that he had wanted Britain to place "some further restraint" on the province. Benjamin Franklin who, as deputy British postmaster in America, had unscrupulously obtained the letters, called for Hutchinson's removal. Hutchinson was

Engrav'd Printed & Sold by PAUL REVERE BOSTON

mobbed (95). But the petition was rejected and Franklin attacked by members of the Privy Council. By this time, news of the Boston Tea Party had reached London. In May, 1773, Lord North had tried to help the East India Company by the Tea Act, by allowing the Company's ships to trade direct with America in order to avoid British customs duties. The Colonists felt they were being offered cheap tea to make them pay the Townshend duty at American ports. North also allowed the Company to sell exclusively to certain American merchants. An increased boycott of tea by the Colonists was the result. On 26th December, 1773, men dressed as Mohawk Indians and organized by Sam Adams, boarded three vessels in Boston harbour and jettisoned tea worth over £9,000 ($45,000) (96). Other "parties", many announced on cards (97), followed. London felt that the time for resolute action had come.

93

94

95

96

97

In March, 1774, the Boston Port Bill was pushed through by George III. The Act closed down the port of Boston until "peace and obedience to the laws" was restored. Three Coercive Acts virtually scrapped the Massachusetts Colonial charter, and stepped up British authority. A soldier, General Thomas Gage, was appointed Governor (98). Many Americans had been shocked by the tea parties. Some, including Benjamin Franklin, felt that the East India Company should be reimbursed for its losses. But after the British reaction, anti-British cartoons became more violent (99, 100, 101). Before the end of August, 1774, British authority was collapsing around Boston. On 3rd September, General Gage began to fortify the city. The Virginian House of Burgesses had been dissolved, but its members gathered at the Raleigh Tavern, Williamsburg, to organize a meeting of States' representatives in defence of American freedom (102). The meetings were to be held

98

99

10

annually. On 5th September, fifty-six delegates met at Carpenter's Hall, Philadelphia (103) for the First Continental Congress of America (104, 105). The Congress tried to restore the situation as it was before the friction with Britain. The Declaration of Rights was adopted as an expression of principles, seeking a recognition of basic human rights supposed to be embodied in the English Constitution. When the English Parliament met at Westminster in November, 1774, George III declared: "The New England governments are in a state of rebellion; blows must decide." Edmund Burke's motion of conciliation was defeated by twenty-seven votes to seventy-eight. Yet the First Continental Congress was at first neither belligerent nor especially republican. It accepted Parliamentary control of commerce abroad, if not commerce at home. But newspapers were openly calling for independence, and local militia forces were being drilled.

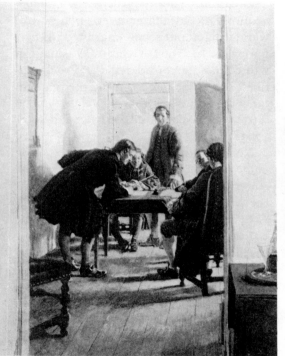

102

104

103

105

CHAPTER FOUR

THE OPENING OF HOSTILITIES

FIGHTING WAS ABOUT to erupt. But out of the confusion of events, noises of protest and anger, recriminations and accusations—what were the main causes of war? Trade was no longer the main issue; indeed, trade grievances were mentioned only once in the Declaration of Independence in 1776. Nor was the war caused by taxation: the Colonists could afford to pay and, in any case, taxes were often repealed. It was not caused only through lack of Colonial representation in the London Parliament. Few Colonists wanted to be represented (James Otis being a notable exception); Americans knew that even if they were represented, it would have little effect. The Colonial slogan "No taxation without representation," should not be exaggerated. The Stamp Act Congress which met in New York in late 1765 to protest about the Stamp Act, explicitly denied that the Colonists wanted representation at Westminster. In any case, few of the British people themselves were represented and yet all were taxed.

Nor was the war primarily caused by Britain's policy toward the new western frontier, despite the Quebec Act. The policy was not unreasonable, and again it was often unenforced. As the Governor of Virginia, Lord Dunmore, wrote: "The established authority of any government in America and the policy at home are both insufficient to restrain the Americans, and they do and will remove as their

avidity and restlessness incite them. They acquire no attachment to place, but wandering about seems engrafted in their nature." In 1767 George Washington wrote that he considered the Proclamation Line "a temporary expedient to quiet the minds of Indians"; at least 30,000 settlers moved west in the five years after 1763.

None of the main events after 1763 alone constituted a *casus belli*; neither the American Act and Currency Act (1764), the Stamp Act (1765), the Declaratory Act stating Parliament's belief in its authority over the Colonies (1776), nor the Restraining Act (1767) forbidding any action by the New York Legislature until it complied with the Quartering Act, the Townshend duties (1767), the Tea Act (1773), the Quebec Act (1774), the Boston Port Bill and the "Coercive Acts" (1774). Alone, none constituted cause for war, but together they made a formidable list and they form a major thread in the tangled reasons for the war.

There were three other main factors. First, the British Government was failing to govern efficiently. Legislation was often ill-timed, clumsy, offensive—and unenforceable. Rather than tyrannical power, executive weakness typified the Crown and the King's ministers. There was vacillation and bowing to pressure groups; there was failure to learn from mistakes, and there was a gross underestimation of the people that Crown and Parliament were dealing with. Inept handling of affairs was evident on the Parliamentary level, aggravated by the quick succession of ministries; it was evident, too, on the civil service level, where departments overlapped and policies were confused; and it was evident in everyday Colonial affairs, managed—or mismanaged—by customs officials, governors, and commissioners.

Another milestone to war was the birth of a nationalist movement in the Thirteen Colonies. Alone, this did not count for much, but with the other factors it helped bring fighting. American nationalism and the radical attitudes that went with it, drew upon the services of powerful propagandists. Although full unity was never achieved among the states, the nationalists did help to unite men of various sections and aims. They made a common appeal to Colonist leaders in North and South alike, whether they were angered most by the Western frontier policy, or by the failure of London at least to consult them before imposing new domestic taxes. To most Colonists, a subject's right to be heard by his rulers was a basic one; it was part of the "natural law" philosophy of the Age of Enlightenment. But neither Parliament nor King would hear or consult them.

But if negotiation had been possible in the early years, it became progressively more difficult. Chances of compromise were destroyed by the short-sightedness of Parliament and King, and partly by the Colonists' own loss of patience and unrealistic demands. The teachings of Locke, translated to the American events by Jefferson and others, were unrealistic; as were Colonial demands for an Anglo-American federation. The lawyer James Otis and Joseph Galloway, among other Americans, proposed something like a "commonwealth" as a possible solution. But these ideas could never have worked. Federal proposals were too radical for Parliament. The idea of a commonwealth link with America was inconceivable, too; William Pitt spoke up for America, but even he would never allow British sovereignty to be questioned. Significantly, Pitt the Liberal was also Pitt the Empire builder. His proposals for reconciliation in 1775 went beyond those of Edmund Burke—and yet he still insisted on colonial subordination to the Parliament, and on Parliament's right to garrison British troops in America. Pitt was a Parliamentarian and the power of Parliament was in no way to be tainted with federalism. While Colonists spoke of natural law and federalism and Parliament talked of its absolute sovereignty, there could be no hope of compromise. Perhaps war was inevitable. America was developing fast and was becoming stronger, all the time growing away from Britain. Yet Britain and America still shared more than a common language: both were proud, both could be arrogant —and each was determined to have its own way.

48 The Massachusetts Provincial Congress prepared for open conflict in 1775. Military supplies were assembled at Worcester and Concord, and the militia put under orders. General Thomas Gage, the British commander, was urged by Lord Dartmouth, Secretary of State for the Colonies, to take action. But Gage knew this would cause a war. So very reluctantly, on 18th April, 1775, he ordered 700 troops to destroy rebel military supplies at Concord. Paul Revere (106) and William Dawes rode ahead to warn the Colonists, who took up arms and began to assemble (107) under Captain John Parker. Just before dawn the British advance guard, under Major John Pitcairn, marched into Lexington. About seventy of Parker's men, lined up on the green, now fell back. Some did turn to go, but took their weapons with them. A shot was fired. Fire was returned and the redcoats charged (108). Captain Parker was killed with seven of his men. One British

107

106

soldier was wounded. At this moment, war began. The main body of British troops arrived. The commander, Lieutenant-Colonel Francis Smith, reluctantly went on to Concord where about 400 American militiamen engaged the British at the North Bridge in a short, violent skirmish (109). During the long return march the British fell prey to ambushes and snipers (110). They barely reached Lexington, and even with reinforcements of 1,200 men had difficulty returning to safety.

The British had lost seventy-three killed, with twenty-six missing. The Americans lost forty-nine, and considered it a victory, commemorated in a painting by Felix Darley, "The First Blow for Liberty, 1776" (111). Next month the Second Continental Congress convened in Philadelphia. John Dickinson's peace petition was scorned in London. Congress rejected Lord North's Conciliatory Resolution, and by August, 1775, Parliament regarded the Colonies in "open and avowed rebellion."

110

111

For nearly two months after Concord, General Gage did not put his few British troops into action. He preferred to concentrate in Boston until help arrived from England. At last, reinforcements arrived, and before the middle of June, 1775, he had about 6,000 men under arms. But on 12th June he wrote to Lord Dartmouth saying that he needed 32,000 men to conquer New England. Thinking that the British were about to seize the offensive, the Americans deployed troops on Breed's Hill and Charlestown peninsula (Boston) to forestall them. Militiamen began to bring up supplies (113) and fortify the area during the night of 16th June (114). Soon after sunrise next morning, British warships opened fire, but without much effect. Gage then ordered General Howe, recently arrived from England, to lead 1,500 men across the harbour, land on the northeast tip of the peninsula (where the militia were not entrenched) and advance up Bunker Hill. At the same time Charlestown

BOSTON

CHARLES TOWN

was bombarded by the British guns (112). But Howe was advancing too slowly, giving the Americans time to strengthen their positions. Calling for reinforcements, Howe attacked the American left flank up the slopes, but the first and second rigidly advancing lines were repulsed. Howe re-formed and Sir Henry Clinton hurried to his aid. Once more the British line advanced in its vulnerable regular formation. Many redcoats fell but the rest staggered on. Short of ammunition, the militia fled, aban-doning their positions (116). But the Patriots lost only 140 men compared to 1,054 British casualties with at least 226 dead. Shocked, General Gage shelved his plan to occupy Dorchester Heights. Meanwhile, the Second Continental Congress had assumed general direction of the American war effort; a Commander-in-Chief was to be appointed. On 15th June, George Washington, a Virginian noted for his bravery during the Seven Years' War, was unanimously chosen (115).

113

112

114 115

116

52 On 2nd July, 1775, George Washington, Commander-in-Chief of the Patriot Army, rode into camp at Cambridge, Massachusetts (117). Although his men were inefficient at first, Washington soon disciplined and organized them. Before long he could escort members of Congress around his Cambridge camp with some confidence in his army (118). Washington knew that the Patriot cause would receive an enormous uplift if only he could drive the British out of Boston. But maps of the city (119) showed how strong the British positions were; also, as they lacked cannons, his men just had to continue the siege in the trenches around the city (120). But cannons for the Patriots were already on their way. By concentrating his army in Boston, Gage could not strengthen the British forces in Quebec; he was anxious for the safety of the key (but vulnerable) garrisons at Ticonderoga and Crown Point which guarded the Hudson River-Lake Champlain-Richelieu

117

118

119

120

River passage between New York City and the St. Lawrence River (121). Before dawn on 10th May, 1775, Patriot forces under Ethan Allen and Benedict Arnold crossed Lake Champlain and reached Fort Ticonderoga (122). The commander of the post, Captain de la Place, was asleep when his guards were overcome and he had to surrender (124), as did Crown Point. On 24th January, 1776, forty-three cannon and sixteen mortars captured at Ticonderoga reached the hands of Washington. On 4th March the guns were placed on Dorchester Heights overlooking Boston (123). The Patriots could now make continued occupation of the city impossible for the British. General Gage had been recalled to London the previous October, so General Howe now had to make the painful choice: to attack Dorchester Heights and risk another Bunker Hill, or withdraw. He decided to withdraw. Defeated and humiliated, the British embarked from Boston in March.

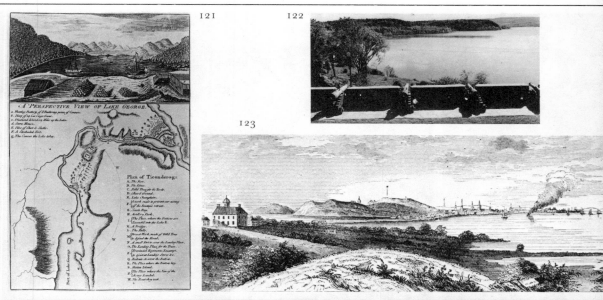

121

122

123

24

In late 1775 sporadic fighting broke out in the South. The Governor of Virginia, Lord Dunmore, was defeated in the battle of Great Bridge, south of Norfolk, Virginia, on New Year's Day, 1776, and forced to retire to Chesapeake Bay. The main British army had been expelled from the Colonies. But it was not yet really a war of independence, although a strong majority of Americans was now calling for one. The Continental Congress, meeting in Independence Hall (125, 126) was in danger of falling behind the wishes of the Colonists. By May, 1776, North Carolina, Massachusetts and Virginia had instructed their delegates to vote for separation from Britain. Tom Paine (127) had created support for the independence movement, blaming George III for the events, saying the Patriots should divorce themselves from Britain and stand up as champions for the rights of mankind. On 7th June, instructed by the Assembly of Virginia, Richard Henry Lee brought in his

125

126

127

128

129 130

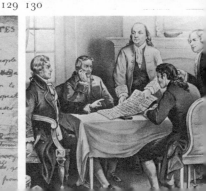

important Congress resolution, that "these United Colonies are, and of right ought to be, free, and independent State." The motion was seconded by John Adams. On 25th June, Congress passed the Allegiance and Treason Resolves, branding the King an enemy; Lee's resolution was approved on 2nd July against some opposition from the Middle Colonies and South Carolina. On 4th July Jefferson's (128) draft of the Declaration of Independence was adopted (129, 130), although New York did not agree to it until 15th July (131). The first to sign was John Hancock, President of Congress (132). Hancock is said to have written his name so that "John Bull" (England) could read it "without his spectacles." Then the rest of the states set their signature to this final break with George III, his Parliament and country (133). Throughout America official British statues were smashed (134) and men hurried to join Washington's army. And across the Atlantic came more English troops.

131

132

133

134

Meanwhile, in Quebec the Patriot Major-General Philip Schuyler moved out from Ticonderoga in late 1775 and besieged the British fort at St. John's (before being replaced by Brigadier-General Richard Montgomery). On 21st November, 1775, after a fifty-six day siege, the Fort surrendered. Now the British at Quebec were threatened: a second force, under Benedict Arnold (136) was moving towards the city, a harsh journey (137). But on 14th November Arnold crossed the St. Lawrence River to occupy the Plains of Abraham before the city. Then, fearing attack, he marched northward a short distance to await reinforcements. At Montreal the British commander barely managed to escape to Quebec before Montreal fell to Richard Montgomery. Montgomery joined forces with Arnold in December and besieged the city. Inside, Sir Guy Carleton and Lieutenant-Colonel Allan McLean prepared strong defences. The attack failed. Mont-

gomery was killed (135) and Benedict Arnold wounded, and command was given for the time being to the Virginian rifleman, Daniel Morgan. The Patriots had to retreat, but outside the city Arnold resumed the blockade with about 600 men. The siege continued into spring, 1776, with the Patriots unable to attack again. At last, the British relieving force under General John Burgoyne appeared. The Americans panicked and many fled. The rest withdrew, via Montreal, to Lake Cham-

plain. There, Schuyler massed the American forces at Ticonderoga and Benedict Arnold strengthened the "fleet" on Lake Champlain. Carleton, who could not move against Ticonderoga until he had defeated this naval force, now built his own fleet, and on 11th October sailed from his position at the north end of the lake. Arnold was outnumbered, and retreated to the south, where in the darkness and fog he managed to dodge the British blockade (138). Carleton spent the winter at St. John's.

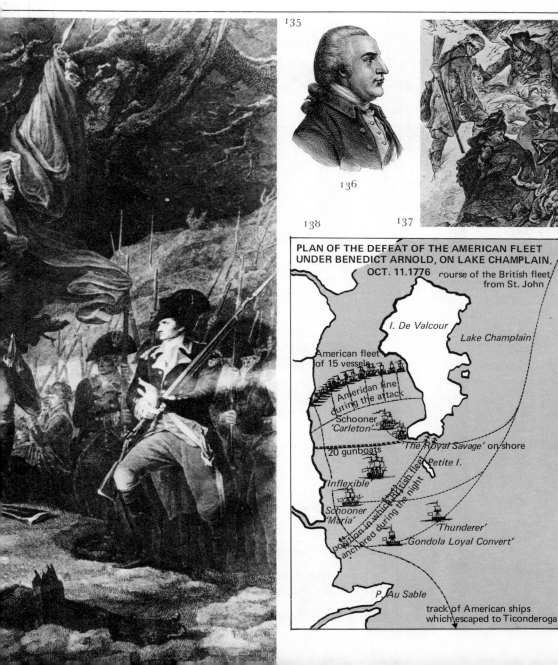

135

136

138

137

PLAN OF THE DEFEAT OF THE AMERICAN FLEET
UNDER BENEDICT ARNOLD, ON LAKE CHAMPLAIN,
OCT. 11.1776   course of the British fleet
from St. John

I. De Valcour   Lake Champlain

American fleet
of 15 vessels

American line
during the attack

Schooner
'Carleton'

The Royal Savage' on shore

20 gunboats   Petite I.

Inflexible

position in which the British Fleet
anchored during the night

Schooner
'Maria'

'Thunderer'

'Gondola Loyal Convert'

P. Au Sable

track of American ships
which escaped to Ticonderoga

While this struggle continued, Britain planned a great concentration of her forces against New England. General Howe was to seize New York and Newport and proceed inland, while his brother Admiral Howe kept up the naval blockade. Carleton was to penetrate into New England after taking Ticonderoga, the two main armies merging to retake Boston, where Washington had evacuated his headquarters (139). Early in 1776 Washington prepared to defend New York City, gathering his largest army, almost 30,000 men. But on 3rd July, the eve of the Declaration of Independence, General Howe seized Staten Island, in the harbour. On 12th July, only slightly damaged by American shore batteries, two British warships sailed up the Hudson River to Tappen Zee. By mid-August General Howe's troops were ready to land. On 21st August, Howe brought his troops ashore on Long Island unopposed. One third of Washington's troops waited on the island, separated from Man-

hattan by the East River. Howe attacked on 27th August, driving Washington's army into a second, stronger, line of defence. The Americans saw they were in danger of being encircled and cut off from escape across the river, and as Howe did not attack at once, Washington managed to slip most of his troops across the East River during the night. Washington doubted whether he could hold New York under British naval bombardment, and so he pulled back still further. On 12th Sep-

tember General Howe tried to stop him with an outflanking movement, but again he was not quick enough; Washington managed to slip away. New York was lost; once more the main British army marched on American soil. The British redcoats disembarked at New York (140) marching victoriously through the city streets (141), while Howe issued proclamations calling for volunteers from the ranks of American Loyalists (142): a sad reversal of Patriot fortunes.

40

142

First Battalion of PENNSYLVANIA LOYALISTS, commanded by His Excellency Sir WILLIAM HOWE, K.B.

ALL INTREPID ABLE-BODIED

HEROES,

WHO are willing to serve His MAJESTY KING GEORGE the Third, in Defence of their Country, Laws and Conſtitution, againſt the arbitrary Uſurpations of a tyrannical Congreſs, have now not only an Opportunity of manifeſting their Spirit, by aſſiſting in reducing to Obedience their too-long deluded Countrymen, but alſo of acquiring the polite Accompliſhments of a Soldier, by ſerving only two Years, or during the preſent Rebellion in America.

Such ſpirited Fellows, who are willing to engage, will be rewarded at the End of the War, beſides their Laurels, with 50 Acres of Land, where every gallant Hero may retire. . . . .

Each Volunteer will receive, as a Bounty, FIVE DOLLARS, beſides Arms, Cloathing and Accoutrements, and every other Requiſite proper to accommodate a Gentleman Soldier, by applying to Lieutenant Colonel ALLEN, or at Captain KEARNY's Rendezvous, at PATRICK TONRY's, three Doors above Market-ſtreet, in Second-ſtreet.

CHAPTER FIVE

THE WAR OF ATTRITION

DESPITE BRITAIN's military recovery in 1776, things were obviously not all going well for her. The American spirit had been underestimated, and the advice and warnings of the British commander, General Gage, had passed unheeded. In 1774 Thomas Gage had told London that he needed at least 20,000 men, stressing that his small force in Boston was quite inadequate. If troops were not sent, Gage declared, it would be wiser to withdraw all forces and British officials, and rely instead upon a strong naval blockade of the North American coast. Repeatedly he asked for more men, first 20,000 then 32,000. "The crisis is indeed an alarming one, and Britain had never more need of wisdom, firmness and union than at this juncture." In early 1776 Sir James Wright cried out to Lord Dartmouth from Virginia: "No troops, no money, no orders or instructions and a wild multitude gathering fast, what can any man do in such a situation. . . Not so much as a ship of war in any kind . . . these things, My Lord, are really *too much*." Whitehall rejected the British commander's warning of the Colonists' strength and determination. Indeed, Gage was virtually accused of cowardice. By December, 1774, pressure against him had so far increased that George III decided to replace him as commander-in-chief by General Sir Jeffrey Amherst. However, early in 1775 it was decided that Gage should stay on as Governor of Massachusetts, and that

Amherst should just take over his military role. This plan failed when Amherst refused to serve in America, and as a result Gage continued as commander. Three Major-Generals, William Howe, Henry Clinton and John Burgoyne, were sent to Boston to assist him, but before they reached America, hostilities had begun. Gage was eventually recalled to London on 10th October, 1775, and Howe replaced him—having the thankless task of leading the British withdrawal from Boston. So, when Britain went to war with America, she had only a small force in the Colonies, and not enough naval strength to blockade the Colonial coasts; all this despite her superior resources.

The orders sent to Gage led inevitably to hostilities. With the war came the risk that France and Spain might side with America, if not actively, then at least by providing equipment, arms and military advisers. By 1774 it was clear to many people that irredeemable mistakes had been made and that Lord North and his ministry were unfit to handle the crisis; the only man who could really do anything about this was George III, and he was as ill-equipped as his prime minister.

When briefing Gage in early 1775 to "do something," even though Gage knew this would mean war, Lord Dartmouth had also said: "It will surely be better that the conflict should be brought on, upon such ground, than in a riper state of rebellion." In other words, the revolt must be crushed before it spread further; if quick action were taken then it could be confined to the Boston area. But Gage knew that if he tried to destroy the rebels in Massachusetts, citizens in the other states would not stand idly by. But Gage was ignored, and Parliament assigned him too few troops even for the Boston operation.

Gage's orders were not posted for forty-five days, perhaps to allow Dartmouth time for eleventh-hour talks with Benjamin Franklin. The orders were finally despatched in February; and yet at the same time, Lord North introduced his Conciliatory Resolution. This, addressed to leading citizens in each of the several Colonies *via* the Governors, promised that if any Colony would vote funds towards Imperial defence, and pay for its own civil officers and judges, Parliamentary taxes would be waived.

The resolution did not go far enough for Lord Rockingham and Lord Chatham, and offended those who wanted a tough policy towards the Colonists. It had a number of flaws. It was not addressed to the Continental Congress; and it implied that a Colony must either tax its citizens "voluntarily," or be taxed by Parliament. It was unacceptable to the Colonists, and in any case the differences with Britain now were more than fiscal. Above all, in Lord North's clumsy fashion, the resolution was put to the Americans after Gage had acted and the war had already begun.

Once the first shots had been fired, Gage seemed to have been proved right. The Colonists had made extensive preparations; the militants had been linked by Committees of Correspondence, launched in Boston in 1772; an infra-structure of revolt had been created. War supplies had already been stockpiled and the militia organized (in a primitive fashion). The handful of redcoats would be lost in a vast territory—which everywhere was hostile. This was no conventional war; fighting fronts were not always clear; traditional army tactics could be disastrous, as at Bunker Hill.

The Colonists' great weapon was the Declaration of Independence. The British may have recovered in 1776, they may have forced back the Patriots in Quebec, they had taken New York; but Howe was soon to learn that territorial conquest was no way to win the war. The Declaration of Independence, unlike New York, could not be captured. It was prized in men's minds and no matter how many square miles the British conquered, the Americans would not be defeated while the spirit of the Declaration lived on. The British would have to learn many lessons. That this was a war for men's minds and not for territory would be the hardest lesson of all.

Already, several cracks had appeared in the British armour. First and foremost there was a divided command: Gage had been replaced in April, 1776, by William Howe, while Sir Guy Carleton stayed in command in Canada. Decisions taken in London took months to reach America, and in London too, opinions were deeply divided. As cartoons illustrated, it seemed to many that George III was riding to a fall (143). Moreover, several senior soldiers including Augustine Keppel (147) refused to serve in America until war was declared with France. The Earl of Sandwich, First Lord of the Admiralty, argued that France was the real enemy, and ships should be kept at home to face threats from over the Channel. The Royal Navy, therefore, could not enforce a strong North American blockade; and despite its superior numbers, the British navy was not unopposed. Americans like Captain John Paul Jones (144), Commodore Esek Hopkins and John Barry caused much harass-

144   143   145   146

ment to the British fleets. In 1778 Jones sailed to the Irish Sea, spiked the guns of a fort at Whitehaven, England, and captured a naval sloop, the *Drake*. A year later, in his armed merchantman the *Bonhomme Richard*, he succeeded in taking prisoner the British ship *Serapis* in the North Sea (145). On land the British soldier (146) fought in the European fashion with rigid close-order lines, often heavily encumbered with equipment; with disastrous results as at Bunker Hill. Tactics should have been shaped by the terrain, which was often harsh and rugged, but the British seemed unwilling to use light infantry. As a result they fell prey to ambushes and sniper fire (148). While the British took up early winter quarters in the European fashion, the Americans carried on fighting. Moreover, the British preferred to stay on the main routes and at their supply depots; but their supply lines became overstretched and vulnerable (149).

147

148

149

The British did have some military advantages. Perennially short of troops in the Thirteen Colonies, they still found it easier than the Patriots to recruit regular soldiers—not in Britain, but in Europe. By autumn 1776, Britain had about 45,000 troops in America, including many German mercenaries. Treaties allowed Britain to put about 30,000 of these "Hessian" soldiers (150) in the field before the end of the war, despite the bitter condemnation by some Members of Parliament. Britain also tried to use the Indians, although the Americans were the first to try to enlist Indian support. These British allies were satirized in contemporary cartoons (151). As most of the Indians were inclined to side with the Crown, the Patriots realized that they would have to fight them as well as redcoats. But the Indians proved unreliable allies, despite hopeful inscriptions on medals awarded

150

151

152

153

to them by the British (152). The Patriots, on the other hand, lacked both finance and industrial power. They were forced to print their own money (153) which often had very little value; Congress issued more than $200 million in Continental bills. At first the Americans could not make ammunition, weapons, gunpowder, or even uniforms, in large enough quantities. British naval supremacy kept out supplies from overseas and allowed Britain to concentrate at points of her own choosing. When General Howe evacuated Boston, George Washington (154) could never be quite certain where he would land next. Washington observed in 1778 that the "maritime resources of Britain are more substantial and real than those of France and Spain united . . . in modern wars the longest course must chiefly determine the event." Washington had to prove himself wrong.

54

Washington was hamstrung by the Colonial militia system. Militiamen served only for a limited length of time, and then went home, even in the middle of a campaign. While the militia scheme had some merits—for example the volunteers made excellent propaganda subjects (155)—it had serious drawbacks. Most members of Washington's first force had only enlisted until the end of the year, and by December many were disappearing; the Patriot commander had to re-form almost a complete army while besieging Boston. Nor were the militiamen always reliable in the face of a British bayonet charge. They operated best in irregular warfare, in skirmishing and in sniping (156). To meet the problem of short-term service, Congress created on 16th September, 1776, the Continentals, men who would serve for three years or for the duration of the war after 1776. The states were to supply no less than eighty-eight battalions; two days after Christmas Washington was empowered

to enlist sixteen more, together with 3,000 cavalrymen, three regiments of artillery and a corps of engineers. In this way he gained the means to win the war (157, 158, 159). However, it took Washington three years to create a uniform system of drill. Difficulties of supply and clothing were not solved until 1782, and even then he lacked clothing enough to delouse his men. But Washington had one supreme advantage. While the British must take the offensive and crush resistance, the Americans had only to keep going until the British tired. Washington did not even have to defeat the enemy in pitched battle; just ensure he was himself not defeated. The American soldiers had far more at stake than their Hessian or even British counterparts: independence. When Washington had the Declaration of Independence read to his troops he was priming and loading the greatest weapon of all (160).

155

156

157

158

159

160

Washington had to hold his army intact at all costs. In 1776 the British had lost an excellent chance to scatter his troops, when Washington evacuated New York, but he escaped with almost his entire army. Washington had been urged to set New York ablaze to deny the British shelter. But Congress disagreed, as did Washington himself. Nevertheless, on 21st September, just after the American army had left, fire swept through about one-fifth of the city, presumably started by Patriots (161, 165).

The damage and the threat of further sabotage decided Howe not to advance up Manhattan Island without reinforcements. Washington now had time to prepare defences in northern Manhattan, and to strengthen Port Washington. But on 12th October Howe resumed the offensive, and within four days Washington was in danger of being trapped on the island. He decided to pull back still further. The main Patriot army withdrew over the Harlem River to the village of White

161

162

PLAN OF BRITISH OPERATIONS IN NEW YORK

N. JERSEY — F. Constitution

N. York

Br. landing
Oct. 12 1776

Am. retreat

American ▭▷

British ■▶

White Plains
Oct. 29 1776

Br. advance

LONG ISLAND

Br. landing
Oct. 16 1776

LONG ISLAND SOUND

miles
0   5   10   20   30   40

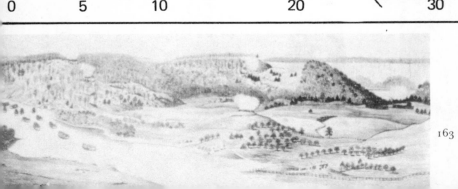

163

164

Plains (162, 163), leaving Port Washington as the only Patriot post in British territory. Howe followed slowly, and did not arrive at White Plains for over a fortnight. Howe then attacked Washington's right wing, deployed on Chatterton's Hill. The Americans fell back, but in good order; the British had the field but the Americans were now in strong hill positions. Howe decided to turn back and attack Port Washington. British warships sailed up the Hudson River to land troops and to bombard the American position, and on the night of 14th November assault stations were taken on the wooded slopes below the fort. On the morrow the American commander, Colonel Magaw, was ordered to surrender. He refused. Next day, British troops scrambled up the steep hillsides (164) supported by fire from the warship *Pearl*. By nightfall, the fort had fallen. Over 2,600 American soldiers were taken prisoner, and Washington, hearing of the defeat, could only continue his retreat.

With only 3,000 men, Washington fled to Newark and back to the Delaware River. With the onset of winter Washington believed that the British pursuit would come to a halt if only he could cross the Delaware. A flotilla of boats was quickly collected. Meanwhile he turned to face the British at Trenton, joined by the Pennsylvania and Maryland militia. But Washington's men were unfit for battle, so he fled once more, ferrying his troops across the icy Delaware River (166). Deciding that the year's campaign was over, Howe took up winter quarters in New Jersey. The Patriots suffered another serious loss: General Lee, moving to join Washington, was captured on 13th December in a house where he had spent the night (167). The rest of his army, reduced to 2,700 men, slipped across the Delaware. Unlike the British, Washington was not finished for the winter. His militiamen would soon be going home, but before they did so, he intended to make two simultaneous attacks

166

167

168

169
170

171

across the Delaware upon Trenton and Bordentown on Christmas night. The first part went well. Washington led 2,400 men through the ice floes on the river above Trenton (168) surprising the 1,500 Hessians in the village (169). Colonel Rall was killed trying to organize them (170). Hessians at Bordentown, however, escaped when part of Washington's force failed to cross the Delaware as planned. In January a British force 6,000-strong advanced on Trenton, commanded by Lord Cornwallis. Washington was outnumbered, and in grave danger; but Cornwallis waited until next morning before attacking. During the night, while camp fires burned to deceive the British, the Americans slipped away to Princeton. In the morning the Patriots attacked Cornwallis from behind. After stiff fighting (171), the British were forced right out of western New Jersey. The Patriots had not collapsed in defeat, and the British were shaken.

In Canada, General John ("Gentleman Johnny") Burgoyne replaced Sir Guy Carleton as British Commander. His army was to push south by way of Lake Champlain, Ticonderoga and Saratoga (172). Howe was to advance up the Hudson, while a third smaller force under Lt.-Colonel Barry St. Leger was to sweep inland from Port Oswego on Lake Ontario. The three were then to converge on Albany. St. Leger met the Mohawk Chief, Joseph Brant, at his village (173). About 1,000 Iroquois, under Brant, joined the British side. Meantime, the Patriot General, Philip Schuyler, was at Albany trying to gather men and supplies; Ticonderoga had only 3,500 Patriot troops commanded by Major-General Arthur St. Clair. Reinforcement was out of the question, and the Americans were exhausted. In addition, St. Clair neglected to fortify Sugar Loaf Hill (Mount Defiance) overlooking the fort. On 4th July, 1777, the British hauled artillery up to the summit,

forcing St. Clair to evacuate the fort. The British could now move on from Ticonderoga to Albany, only seventy miles away. But the road was extremely bad, winding through thick forests and over endless streams. Schuyler and his men blocked the road as they went, felling trees and diverting streams. Burgoyne did not reach Fort Edward and the Hudson River until 29th July. There he made camp (174) to rest his men and await his cannon. Meanwhile he ordered Colonel Friedrich Baum to raid into the Green Mountain country. Confronted with a strong Patriot force at Bennington, Baum was attacked and killed, and the remnants of his force either fled or were captured (175). The British force under St. Leger had advanced down the Mohawk Valley, and had besieged Fort Stanwix near Oriskany (later named Fort Schuyler) on 2nd August. American reinforcements were ambushed and forced to turn back. The situation for the Patriots looked desperate indeed.

But help was coming to Fort Stanwix: a relief force under Benedict Arnold. Arnold persuaded a half-witted Tory (Hans Yest Schuyler) to warn St. Leger that the Patriots were advancing with 3,000 men—instead of about 1,000. The deception worked. St. Leger's Indians fled and the British General retreated. Horatio Gates (176) now took up the Patriot command in Canada, and had to face Burgoyne. Burgoyne attacked on 19th September, trying to outflank the American left wing, but he found it reinforced by riflemen led by Daniel Morgan (177). His own formations were broken up in the thick forest. Morgan went in hot pursuit of General James Hamilton at Freeman's Farm. Weary and outnumbered, the British retired. On 7th October Burgoyne sent forward 1,500 men into the battle known variously as the second of Freeman's Farm, Bemis Heights, or Stillwater. Many British fell dead or wounded, and Burgoyne retreated to Saratoga under

176

177

179

178

cover of darkness. There he faced the Patriots. The American army numbered over 17,000 men with the militia coming to join Gates' force. Clearly the British relief force under Sir Henry Clinton could never arrive in time. On 12th October Burgoyne resolved to flee, only to find himself trapped on every side. Gates demanded total surrender. On 14th October, 1777, Burgoyne agreed to order his men to lay down arms, so long as they could sail home to England, never again to serve in America.

Gates accepted. Three days later Burgoyne formally surrendered (178), and gave himself up as a prisoner. Saratoga was a crucial landmark in the American revolution. The news shocked London. Earlier that year the Continental Congress had approved America's first national flag. According to tradition, the design was created by a flagmaker, Betsy Ross (Mrs. Elizabeth Griscom) (179); the first flag was made in her house in Arch Street, Philadelphia (180).

180

After New Jersey had collapsed in 1776, the British General Sir William Howe decided to attack Philadelphia. This would leave Burgoyne unprotected in the north, but messages from Burgoyne in July, 1777, showed that he was well placed. That month, Howe sailed with his men in 260 vessels south for Chesapeake Bay, from where he marched cross-country toward Philadelphia. As Washington's forces were weakened by sending reinforcements north after the fall of Ticonderoga, Washington set up defensive positions with 11,000 men at Brandywine Creek, across Howe's overland route to the Patriot capital. Posters in the capital told of Howe's progress and called men to arms (181). Howe now divided his force, sending out two flanking movements. Almost surrounded, Washington pulled back—but not with sufficient speed. He suffered more than a thousand casualties, and could not hold the British from the capital. The Continental Congress had

In COUNCIL of SAFETY,

PHILADELPHIA, December 8, 1776.

SIR,

THERE is certain intelligence of General Howe's army being yesterday on its march from Brunswick to Princetown, which puts it beyond a doubt that he intends for this city.—This glorious opportunity of signalizing himself in defence of our country, and securing the Rights of America forever, will be seized by every man who has a spark of patriotic fire in his bosom. We entreat you to march the Militia under your command with all possible expedition to this city, and bring with you as many waggons as you can possibly procure, which you are hereby authorized to impress, if they cannot be had otherwise—Delay not a moment, it may be fatal and subject you and all you hold most dear to the ruffian hands of the enemy, whose cruelties are without distinction and unequalled.

By Order of the Council,

DAVID RITTENHOUSE, Vice-President.

To the COLONELS or COMMANDING OFFICERS of the respective Battalions of this STATE.

TWO O'CLOCK, P.M.

THE Enemy are at Trenton, and all the City Militia are marched to meet them.

181   182
       183

184

already escaped, and on 25th September, 1777, Howe victoriously marched in. Washington determined to strike back. In anticipation, Howe posted 9,000 men at Germantown to parry the blow; but during the night of 5th October Washington attacked, hoping to surprise the British. But an outlying British position gave stiff resistance at Chew House in Germantown (182), allowing the rest of the British force precious minutes to prepare. Even so, the Patriots burst through the main line at one point, before retiring into confusion because of fog. Howe retired to comfortable winter quarters in Philadelphia. Washington went to Valley Forge. The winter of 1777–78 was grim for the American army, plagued by shortages of clothing, food and equipment. Twice the soldiers nearly starved (183, 184); many deserted. The Patriots all knew that only twenty miles away the British were eating and carousing in the American capital.

Although the Patriot army suffered wretchedly during the winter months, overall American prospects were bright. In the comfort of Philadelphia, Sir William Howe was not happy. In London, Lord George Germain had begun to criticize him, and Howe himself had asked to resign as early as October. In Paris the impact of Saratoga was decisive. King Louis XVI (185) was advised that the American rebellion now offered even better prospects of striking out against Britain. But as Britain seemed about to offer a compromise peace, France must act quickly. The American ambassador Benjamin Franklin pressed hard for a French agreement, finding time to play the gallant to influential Parisian ladies to win their support (186). On 6th February, 1778, a Franco-American treaty was signed and handed to Franklin (187). France and America promised to help one another, and not to make peace without the other's consent. Washington received this news on 1st May,

1778, and informed his army four days later. The treaty was enthusiastically welcomed, and medals of commemoration were struck (188, 189). Never had the army been in better shape. In February, as the snows began to melt at Valley Forge, a better camp was constructed (190). In the same month a military expert, Baron von Steuben (191), arrived from Europe and took over the training of troops, particularly in the art of co-ordinated manoeuvring. Finally, to strengthen the military leadership, it was arranged that General Charles Lee, captured *en route* to join Washington over the Delaware in late 1776, should be returned to the Patriots in exchange for General Prescott, captured by the Americans on Rhode Island. The Patriot army, hardened by experience, had now received the final polish. Her soldiers waited in readiness for the next season of war.

CHAPTER SIX

THE CLOSING YEARS OF WAR

THE WAR HAD ebbed and flowed, but once again the tide ran strongly for the American rebels. The longer the war lasted the harder it would be for Britain to win. Moreover, Britain was still making serious mistakes. She had failed to take advantage of her greater resources, and the problems of command had not been resolved. Howe had replaced Gage in April, 1776, in preference to Carleton who would have been the better choice. But some of Carleton's political views upset the British ministers; he was even guilty of showing Americans some respect. So Howe was chosen, and yet he was often over-hesitant. When he allowed Washington to evacuate New York in September, 1776, he could have used his brother, Admiral Howe, to trap the American army between the Harlem and Hudson Rivers. But he delayed too long; and his pursuit of the Americans on their way back to White Plains was of no avail. Now Howe was about to leave his dubious comfort in Philadelphia and return home. It was not before time.

Then had come Saratoga and the French alliance—and the loss of Burgoyne's army into Virginian and Pennsylvanian prison camps after the Continental Congress had repudiated the Saratoga Convention. The French had, in fact, been helping the Americans for some months, but the Patriots had not found it easy to obtain French signatures to an official treaty, despite the sympathy of Frenchmen like Etienne François, Duc de Choiseul. Choiseul had urged Louis XV to take action, but the King had not been convinced. Then, in 1774, Louis XV had died. His grandson and heir, Louis XVI, had hesitated too.

Louis XVI's Foreign Minister, Charles Gravier (Comte de Vergennes) had, like Choiseul, wanted France to play a full part in the Anglo-American conflict. He was supported by the influential Baron de Beaumarchais, author of *The Barber of Seville* and *The Marriage of Figaro* and a French secret agent in London. Vergennes urged Louis to give secret aid to the Patriots, and in March, 1776, also persuaded the Spanish Foreign Minister, the Marquis de Grimaldi, to agree that if France helped America so would Spain. If the war continued until both sides were exhausted, Spain and France could step in and seize the spoils. On 2nd May, 1776, Louis XVI at last gave his assent. Beaumarchais had set up a pseudo merchant house in Paris which stockpiled weapons, ammunition and other supplies and secretly shipped them off to America. In 1776 and 1777 French aid amounted to four million livres. Besides the supplies, including gunpowder which was in short supply, a number of Frenchmen sailed across the Atlantic to fight. Among them were the Marquis de Lafayette and Louis Le Begue de Presle Duportail.

In December, 1776, Benjamin Franklin, Silas Deane and Dr. Arthur Lee acted as

Patriot envoys in Paris, instructed by Congress to secure official diplomatic recognition of America. But the trio did not have an easy path. Arthur Lee (brother of Richard Henry Lee) rightly guessed that Deane and Sir Edward Bancroft, the envoy's secretary, were in British pay.

When news came of Saratoga, Vergennes was ready to act, provided the Spaniards acted with the French. Britain, wishing to avert an alliance between France and America, now let it be known through Deane that she was about to offer generous peace terms. But this had just the opposite effect. It made Vergennes determined to act even more quickly. On 17th December, 1777, he told the American envoys that France would formally recognize the United States of America. Then he heard that although the Spanish Ambassador at Paris, the Comte de Aranda, supported him, his superiors in Madrid did not. Vergennes went ahead just the same, and signed the treaties on 6th February, 1778. Lord North's Conciliatory Resolutions of February, offering a compromise peace, arrived too late.

War between Britain and France was now a certainty; but the first shots were not fired for another four months. Vergennes continued to try and bring the Spaniards in, offering Minorca, the Floridas and Jamaica as bait. All offers were refused. The French minister then promised that France would help Spain recover Gibraltar, and a secret convention was signed in April, 1779. Spain then told Britain to accept her mediation in the Anglo-French struggle, or else risk Spanish attack. As Spain had expected, the offer of mediation was thrown out. Spain now went to war.

The following year, after Britain had searched and impounded a number of neutral warships, several neutral countries signed a League of Armed Neutrality against Britain. So hostile was Dutch conduct toward Britain, that Britain declared war on the Dutch in 1780. Britain now had America, France, Spain and the Netherlands ranged against her. But the amount of official help the Patriots gained from their allies must not be exaggerated. Independence could still have been achieved without formal intervention by France.

Some 9,000 French troops fought in America, of which the most valuable were to be those taking part in the siege of Yorktown. But the French entry created a more intense war effort in Britain than had existed before. Moreover, the Patriots found it hard to fight side by side with the French. The French fleet kept moving off for the West Indies; joint operations were to fail many times, partly through bad luck, partly through difficulties in reaching clear agreement. Spanish help was even less effective and the League of Armed Neutrality never actually came to blows with Britain. The main burden of war still had to be shouldered by the American Patriots.

The Patriots still had to clear many rocks from their path. Unity still eluded them: many of them disagreed about the government of the new nation. Clearly, if the war did finish with an American victory, a major struggle would break out between the various political groups. In the meantime, the bitterest clash was between the Americans who were Revolutionaries and those still loyal to George III. Blood was constantly shed between them, and the latter, regarded as traitors, were dealt with most harshly. The black market was also a problem. The blockade brought about a prosperous black market, in which some merchants increased their wealth six-fold. Merchants were warned not to inflate prices unduly (192), but some inflation was bound to occur. Worst hit was the Army and all fixed-income groups, as the paper currency plummetted in value (193, 194). Some farmers grew rich from the high prices paid for their produce by both armies, but others were ruined by the

All Friends to Liberty, and, the Good, of their Country.—

Are Desire'd to take Notice, that there is men in this City, that, in Order to Ruin our Cause, and to Distress us as much as possible, has Lately Consulted together, and Did Actualy Raise the price, of the most Nesesary Articles, of Life — on the News of the Enemys apearing on our Coast and if and, orderly, Malitia will Bring them Before the Civil Magestrates, —

1779 May

I will point out and appear against them

N B
Some Nesesary article has Rose double the price, in three weeks if these men pass with impunity, where will it

Terra Firma

Ends —

war. Although small by later standards, the armies still caused extensive damage to property, and many farmers destroyed their crops to prevent the enemy getting them (198). But now the Americans were no longer alone in their fight; the British were beginning to panic. Some Frenchmen (195) had already been serving unofficially in America, like the young Marquis de Lafayette, a Major-General in America at the age of nineteen (196). A French fleet was likely to appear on the American horizon at any moment. The British feared that this fleet would smash the blockade and, worse still, pin down the British Army and Royal Navy vessels in North America, while the British West Indies were plundered. Indeed, a powerful French force including eleven ships of the line and commanded by the Comte d'Estaing (197) reached the North American coast on 8th July, 1778.

195

196

197

198

Meanwhile General Howe had resigned and in May, 1778, General Sir Henry Clinton (199) took command. In view of the French threat, Clinton was told to evacuate Philadelphia and mass his troops in New York. By late June the British had left the Continental capital. Part of the British army sailed north, while the rest under Clinton marched overland. Burdened with 1,500 baggage vehicles, Clinton's force made slow progress and was intercepted at Monmouth Courthouse. General Lee, now back with the Patriot army, was ordered to attack the enemy rearguard with 4,000 men. He advanced, but was opposed by the British main force, and was forced to withdraw. General Washington rode forward and reprimanded Lee for retreating (200). Lee is said to have answered: "Sir, these troops are not able to meet British grenadiers." Washington angrily shouted: "Sir, they are able and by God they shall do it!" Taking command himself, Washington repulsed two British

199

200

201

counter-attacks (201), including a cavalry charge by Clinton. Neither side gained ground and, in the battle, one "Molly Pitcher" (so-called because she carried water to the troops) took her wounded husband's place at the guns (202). Exhausted by the heat, the two sides drew apart. Clinton withdrew during the night to New York, and Washington followed, taking up positions outside the city. General Lee was now court-martialled by Washington. Charges against him were far from proven, but he was found guilty and suspended from army command for twelve months; he never fought again. Washington's land forces were augmented by d'Estaing's French fleet lying at anchor outside New York. It was intended that the French warships should force their way in, but Admiral Howe's British fleet was well prepared inside the harbour, and the waters at the entrance were too shallow for the largest French vessels. The plan had to be given up and a new target chosen.

The Americans and French commanders now agreed to attack the British garrison at Newport, Rhode Island. D'Estaing's fleet arrived offshore on 29th July, 1778, and the Patriot General John Sullivan advanced with 10,000 men. The plight of the British commander, Sir Robert Pigot, and his 3,000 men was desperate. Admiral Howe, with fewer warships than d'Estaing, sailed to Pigot's support. Luckily for the British a storm scattered the two fleets off Rhode Island, and ships from Admiral John Byron's newly arrived squadron came to Howe's rescue. D'Estaing withdrew to Boston, and the position at Newport was reversed. General Sullivan had to pull back. Admiral Howe now sailed back in triumph to England while Byron went to try and trap the French fleet. D'Estaing slipped away for the West Indies, and once again Washington was deserted. But Clinton was still held in New York, and his only hope of defeating the larger Patriot army was to entice Washington

203

204   205

into a costly mistake outside the city. He posted forces up the Hudson River to capture a lightly defended American post at Stony Point: here was the bait. Washington refused to fall into the trap, and merely moved further up river to West Point (203). Here, he swiftly turned and sent forces back to Stony Point, launching a surprise attack under General (Mad Anthony) Wayne (204). During the night of 15th–16th July Wayne's men filed up the hillside, stormed the fort and took it after vicious hand-to-hand fighting (205), with Wayne continuing to direct his men despite his wounds (206). It was a brilliant prestige victory. Another American surprise attack followed soon afterwards, led by Henry Lee, the father of Robert E. Lee. Striking before sunrise on 19th August he seized the British post at Paulus Hook, New Jersey, and hurried back with prisoners before British reinforcements came on the scene.

Stalemate overshadowed the North from the end of 1779 until the summer of 1780. In June, 1780, Baron von Knyphausen, whom Clinton had left in command in New York while he visited the South, sent a British force into New Jersey; this was driven back by militiamen. When the Baron tried again on 23rd June he was opposed by Nathanael Greene, but this time the Patriots were forced back at a skirmish near Springfield, New Jersey. On 10th July the French fleet, commanded by the Chevalier de Ternay, returned with nearly 5,000 troops under the Comte de Rochambeau. These troops came ashore at Newport. With the aid of French seapower, Washington believed that he could renew the offensive. But first a great war scandal burst. Benedict Arnold, the brave and brilliant Patriot Major-General, was found to be a traitor. Clinton's deputy Adjutant-General, Major John André,

207

210 211

was captured while returning from seeing Arnold (207). Papers found on him revealed that for sixteen months Arnold had secretly corresponded with the British, and promised to help them capture West Point. Had he felt dissatisfied about promotion, or lived too extravagantly at his wife's home in Philadelphia (208)? His motives were obscure. Colonel Benjamin Tallmadge (209) escorted André to Washington's headquarters at Tappan for trial (210). As André had been arrested in civilian clothes, he was branded as a spy and sentenced to death on the gallows. Arnold escaped to a British ship in the Hudson (211, 212). He was paid his price, £6,000 ($30,000), and the British reluctantly made him a general. Today a strange monument to him stands at Saratoga, New York: a carved stone boot. Arnold had twice been wounded in the leg by the British; it was his only American virtue.

212

The British now shifted the battle zone to the South, and clashes between the main armies in the North dwindled. But in the meantime another vicious struggle continued: the Indian operations in the West, where atrocities like the Wyoming massacre (213) were frequent. Operations were conducted against the Patriots on the long western frontier by the Indian tribes, supported by British money and by British troops. According to the Declaration of Independence, the British had "endeavoured to bring on the inhabitants of our frontiers the merciless Indian savages; whose known rule of warfare is an undistinguished destruction of all ages, sexes and conditions." The British were more hated for their use of Indians than for anything else. Brutal savages were shown as murdering gallant Patriot soldiers (214). In unleashing the Indians, the British had much to answer for, although they

often tried to check their hiring. Indeed, the British sometimes received more than they bargained for; rewarded by bounties, the Indians were liable to slaughter participants on both sides. British officials tried to organize the Indians by riding into the frontier territory to meet the Chiefs and to pay for the use of their men (215, 216). Lord Dunmore tried to bring savages into operation on the frontiers of Virginia early in the war; and even before the war the British Indian Superintendent, John Stuart, had tried to organize Indians to fight against the rebels, telling them to stay quiet until British troops appeared. Most of the Indian fighting lacked cohesion. One or two operations became full-scale campaigns, however, including the bloody raids led by John Butler, and the equally violent counter-offensives against the Indians and their British leaders by Patriots like General John Sullivan.

214

215

213

216

General Frederick Haldiman succeeded Carleton as Governor of Canada in 1778. Haldiman feared a new Patriot offensive against Quebec, and that the French Canadians, like France, would ally with the Americans. Doubting whether he could protect his territory with the troops at hand, he supplemented his forces with British sympathizers and Iroquois. In June, 1778, Haldiman sent out Colonel John Butler with a group of 400 British supporters and 500 Iroquois from Port Niagara to enter northern Pennsylvania along the Susquehanna River. They totally devastated the valley. The Patriot Zebulon Butler was defeated trying to stop them, and those captured or left wounded were scalped and tortured. Settlers were attacked and slaughtered (217). The survivors galloped on ahead to warn others (218). Forts at Kingston and Wilkesborough were overrun by Butler's Indians, and the prisoners burnt to death. Joseph Brant, the Mohawk

218

217

Chief, raided Patriot territory two months later. German Flats, a village on the Mohawk River, was encircled by his force of 150 Indians and 300 whites. The villagers fled into a church and two small forts, and most buildings were consumed in flames. In November, Brant returned with Captain Walter Butler (Colonel Butler's son) leading about 500 Indians and 200 Rangers. They invaded Cherry Valley, west of Albany. Inhabitants fled to a stockade and, although some were killed, they held off the attackers. Washington decided to lay waste the Iroquois country and a large body of Patriots under Major-General John Sullivan marched into the territory in August, 1779. After an abortive ambush by Brant and Walter Butler at Newtown (219), Sullivan's men destroyed forty-one Iroquois villages (220). Indians were scalped, and even skinned alive. Men and women were burned at the stake. As reprisal followed reprisal, these actions merged into one unending feud.

219

94

The most famous Indian fighter was George Rogers Clark, of Kentucky County, Virginia (222), whose fame grew out of Indian attacks on the Ohio Valley in 1777 and early 1778. The Indians were supported by Lt.-Colonel Henry ("Hair-Buyer") Hamilton at Detroit. Twice in 1778 the Patriots tried to reach Detroit to attack Hamilton and stop the raids, but both times they failed. Clark, with Virginia Assembly funds, then planned an expedition against Kaskaskia, Cahokia, Vincennes and other Illinois villages before crossing into Detroit. Clark had approval and instructions from Patrick Henry and embarked down the Ohio River with only 175 men (221). Even after the 120-mile overland march he took Kaskaskia without trouble. Cahokia, sixty miles farther upstream, was also successfully attacked. Meanwhile Henry Hamilton came out of Detroit to meet the threat. Marching 600 miles in ten weeks he reached Vincennes in a snowstorm on 17th December, before

221 223

moving farther on to engage Clark. But at Kaskaskia, instead of preparing defences, Clark trekked overland, crossing 240 miles of terrible country in deplorable weather to forestall Hamilton. With 170 men, he set out early in February, 1779. The going was hard, and his men suffered terribly from frost-bite and exhaustion; but they reached the Wabash River opposite Vincennes, where Hamilton had strongly defended the stockade. Clark crossed the Wabash to attack (223), marching his men into the village in two columns, to make the force appear larger. Most of Hamilton's Indians deserted. Clark besieged the stockade, and on 25th February Hamilton surrendered (224). Clark sent the British officer under escort to Williamsburg and ruled as virtual dictator in the area, although Indian raids in Ohio never entirely ceased. Clark never reached Detroit. He proposed the expedition again in 1780, but Virginia faced invasion and could not help.

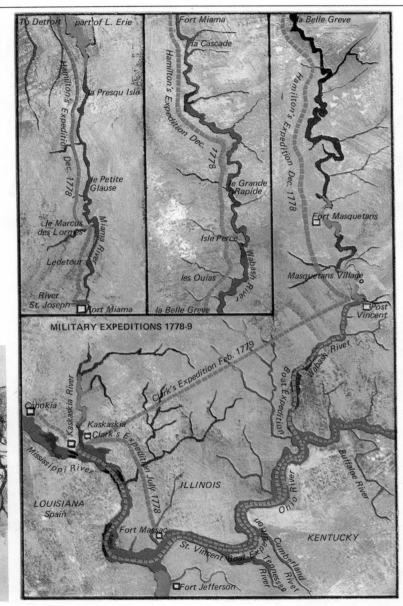

MILITARY EXPEDITIONS 1778-9

During this time the war in the South had assumed most importance. Southern Patriots had not been troubled for nearly two years—ever since Clinton had made an attack on Sullivan's Island, which guarded the entrance to Charleston Harbour (225). The Patriot commander, General Charles Lee, had thrown up defences and mustered troops (226) in Charleston itself (227); Colonel William Moultrie, commanding the fort on Sullivan's Island, had led the main defence. On 28th June, nine British ships had bombarded the fort, and the Patriots had responded, heavily damaging the fleet (228). In 1778 the British attacked Savannah. In November, Clinton sent 3,500 men under Lt.-Colonel Archibald Campbell to capture the city, which they did. The British pushed inland, taking Augusta at the end of January and gaining all Georgia. General Benjamin Lincoln crossed the Savannah River to counterattack. Meanwhile, General Sir George Prevost marched his

225

226

227

British force against Charleston, arriving on 12th May, to demand its surrender. Knowing that Lincoln was on his way, the authorities delayed and Prevost had to fall back to Savannah. The Patriots moved against Prevost. D'Estaing arrived with the French fleet and Savannah was placed under siege (229). But the Patriots failed to smash the defences in October, and d'Estaing had to sail again for West Indian waters. The British renewed the offensive against Charleston. By the end of March the city was almost surrounded, with British warships under Admiral Marriot Arbuthnot blockading the coast (230). On 10th April, 1780, Lincoln was asked to surrender. He refused, but the last escape route, to the north, was blocked by Lt.-Colonel Banastre Tarleton on 12th May. Lincoln had to accept British terms. Charleston's defence had been hopeless from the outset, and British rule now seemed to be tightly restored in the two southernmost American states.

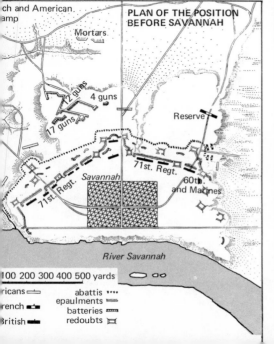

PLAN OF THE POSITION BEFORE SAVANNAH

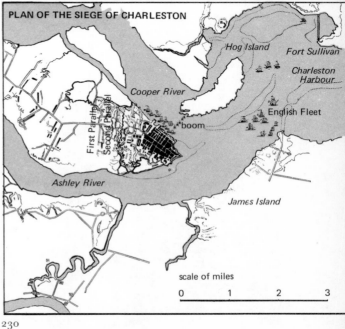

PLAN OF THE SIEGE OF CHARLESTON

America launched a counter-offensive to re-take the Southern states. Horatio Gates became commander of the Patriot forces in the South. In July 1780, he joined forces with Baron de Kalb, a French officer. On 13th August, the army camped thirteen miles from the British post at Camden, South Carolina. That same day Lord Cornwallis reached Camden with British reinforcements. In the battle three days later (231), the American militia moved first, but a bayonet charge failed and the men wavered in disorder (232). Cornwallis at once attacked and broke the American line; Baron de Kalb was killed and the Patriots routed (233). With only 700 men left, Gates retired to Hillsborough. Cornwallis now moved on to Charlotte, not far from Gates. But Major Patrick Ferguson, moving from Fort Ninety-Six in South Carolina was attacked by irregulars and forced to make a stand at King's Mountain. But before help arrived, Patriots had overrun Ferguson's

American Troops
British Troops

British in pursuit

Americans in flight

Americans drawn up in order of battle

advance of the British

British drawn up in order of battle

PLAN OF THE BATTLE OF CAMDEN

231

233

position. On his way to help, Sir Banastre Tarleton (234) returned to Cornwallis who was also under attack. The British had to retreat from the Patriots. In December, 1780, Gates was replaced by Nathanael Greene (235), who divided his army to give greater flexibility, placing the second section under Daniel Morgan's command. Morgan clashed with Colonel Tarleton at Cowpens, South Carolina, on New Year's Day, 1781. Morgan planned his defences well; two lines of riflemen were stationed in front of the main line. They were to fire two volleys and then flee. Cavalrymen were hidden in the woods. The illusion worked. Tarleton's dragoons chased the fleeing riflemen, only to be confronted by Morgan's cavalry under Colonel William Washington, cousin of the General (236). The rest of the British found themselves attacking the main Patriot line, imagining that the strongest enemy position had been overrun. Tarleton barely made his escape with 140 horsemen.

234

235

236

Determined to take revenge, Cornwallis unsuccessfully chased Morgan northward. Greene united the two sections of his army at Guilford Courthouse, and crossed the Dan River into North Carolina in mid-February, 1781. Stopped by the swollen river, Cornwallis had to make his way back to his supply base at Hillsborough. In March, Greene ordered his army over the river again. On the 14th, he took up positions at Guilford Courthouse, deploying his men in the same pattern Morgan had used at Cowpens (237). When the sun rose next morning, Cornwallis attacked (238). The first British assault lines were shattered by the concentrated fire of the militiamen, but they bravely re-formed and advanced again. Faced by a line of British bayonets, many of the American militia fled. If Greene had thrown in all his reserves he might still have won, but the cost of failure would have been disastrous. To withdraw was safer. Cornwallis might claim a British victory, but he had lost more

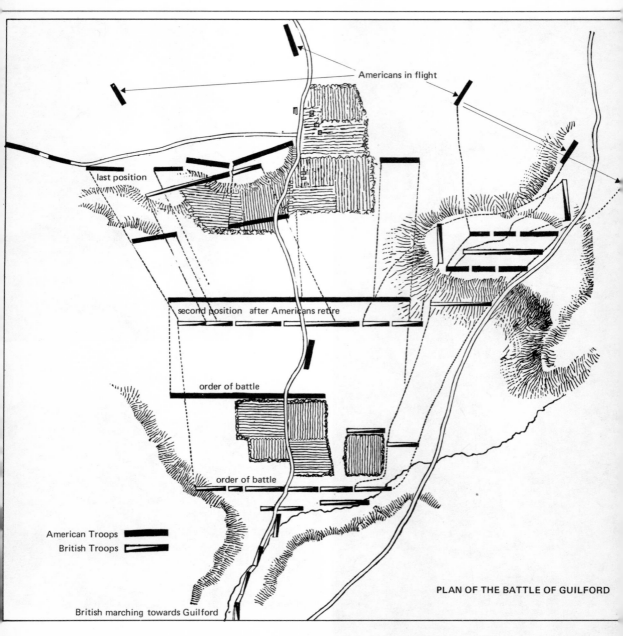

Americans in flight

last position

second position after Americans retire

order of battle

order of battle

American Troops

British Troops

PLAN OF THE BATTLE OF GUILFORD

British marching towards Guilford

men than the Americans. His army weakened, he withdrew eastward toward the coast and Wilmington. Greene was now free to engage the remaining British forces in Georgia and South Carolina, and attacked the forts ringing Charleston and Savannah. Fort Watson was taken on 23rd April. The British area commander, Lord Rawdon (239), advanced to protect his posts and clashed with Greene on 25th April on the long ridge of Hobkirk's Hill, a mile from Camden. The two sides each counted about 1,500 men. The initial British attack, mainly with cavalry, was parried by Colonel Washington's dragoons, but only after the American left flank had been dislodged. Rawdon himself was enmeshed in the American counterattack, but the British recovered and the militiamen fell back in disorder. Greene had to retreat, covered by Washington's dragoons (240). Rawdon withdrew towards Charleston with the British force.

239

238

240

Greene decided to attack Fort Ninety-Six. The garrison held out for a month before its evacuation was ordered by Rawdon early in July, 1781 (241). The British commander left for England, appointing Lt.-Colonel Alexander Stuart in his place. With 2,000 men each, Greene and Stuart manoeuvred for position, and on 8th September they faced one another at Eutaw Springs (242). Under Greene's onslaught the British troops took to their heels, but Greene's troops found rum in the British camp and, while they caroused, the British re-formed and attacked. Greene had to withdraw. But again British casualties outstripped the American, and Stuart made his way back toward Charleston. Eutaw Springs was the last major clash in the deep South. The British could only occupy the coastal towns, and finally on 14th December, 1782, Charleston itself was evacuated. Greene and his men triumphantly paraded through the city streets. Fighting had shifted north-

241

242

244 243

ward. Cornwallis was commander in Virginia (243), and British raids under Benedict Arnold ravaged the countryside. Washington sent 1,200 men to the area, under the Marquis de Lafayette (244) and early in March, 1781, the French fleet sailed from Newport, Rhode Island, to trap Arnold in the Chesapeake. Sir Henry Clinton in New York, fearing British vulnerability in Virginia, sent a British fleet to follow the French. They met off Chesapeake Bay, and the French were forced to withdraw. Hearing that a powerful French fleet had left Brest on the French coast, Clinton wanted to mass his troops in New York and asked Cornwallis to send him the bulk of his force. Cornwallis refused, and against his better judgement, Clinton let Cornwallis keep his army in the Virginia area. He was told to set up positions on the peninsula between the James and York Rivers. And there by August, 1781, the British began to make defensive earthworks (245).

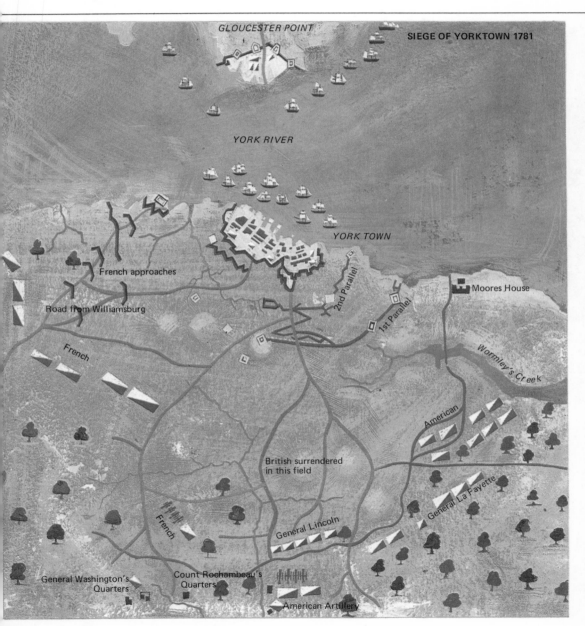

GLOUCESTER POINT

SIEGE OF YORKTOWN 1781

YORK RIVER

YORK TOWN

French approaches

2nd Parallel

1st Parallel

Moores House

Road from Williamsburg

French

Wormley's Creek

American

British surrendered in this field

General La Fayette

French

General Lincoln

General Washington's Quarters

Count Rochambeau's Quarters

American Artillery

245

All had not been well in Washington's main army. Washington had gone into winter quarters on 1st December, 1780, with troops of the Pennsylvania Line based at Morristown, the New Jersey line at Pompton, and the New England men at West Point and other posts along the Hudson River. The General himself based his own quarters at New Windsor, New York. The men, though better provided for than in the previous winter, still suffered hardships. They were weary from war; food and shelter were scarce; the winter was exceptionally hard. Many complained of arrears of pay, or the issue of worthless Continental paper money. Some troops demanded their release claiming that they had served their three-year enlistment period. They were reminded that they had agreed to stay till the end of the war. Finally about 1,700 men of the Pennsylvania Line mutinied at the start of 1781 (246). Their immediate grievance was the whisper that new recruits were being paid

247

246

hard currency. Refusing to obey their officers, the mutineers marched off toward Philadelphia to place their demands before Congress. Washington agreed that the mutineers had some justice in their claims, and a sergeants' committee was told by officials that all those soldiers who had enlisted for three years only, and who had not received a bounty or had re-enlisted, would be discharged. The men returned to duty. But later in January troops of the New Jersey Continentals at Pompton also rebelled. Loyal New Englanders sent by Washington surrounded the dissidents and arrested the ringleaders. The troubles quietened, although restlessness still continued. It was up to Washington to unite his Army again, to revitalize the "glorious spirit of 1776" as it was depicted in this painting (247). The crisis in the American Army passed, and Washington was ready for the final great offensive. Picture (248) shows officers of his army.

At last, American and French combined operations began to work smoothly. Washington met the French commander Jean-Baptiste-Donatien de Vimeur Rochambeau at the latter's headquarters in Wethersfield, Connecticut (249) in May, 1781, and Admiral François Joseph Paul de Grasse (250) was sailing to America *via* the West Indies with a powerful French fleet. It was decided to engage Clinton at New York City, and on 14th June the French army marched out of Newport to join the American forces at White Plains on 10th July. But Cornwallis was digging in at Yorktown. Rochambeau persuaded Washington that the chances of victory were even greater there, and the Comte de Grasse was to block Chesapeake Bay and the British sea escape. Washington agreed to be there in August. While Lafayette and the main American and French forces marched south to join Washington, men were posted outside New York to make Clinton believe that he was still the main

249

250

25

target. The British admiral George Rodney (252) in the Caribbean failed to stop de Grasse who sailed north. Rodney turned for England, sending too few warships northward after the French. De Grasse arrived at the entrance to Chesapeake Bay on 30th August, with 3,000 French regulars. These joined Lafayette in the trenches outside Yorktown. Cornwallis was surrounded. And the British were soon to learn the French troops were unlike their cartoon caricatures (251). Washington's army also joined the besieging force, and Cornwallis now faced an enemy over 16,000 strong. His only hope was the defeat of the French navy. Sailing for the Chesapeake Admiral Sir Thomas Graves engaged de Grasse on 5th September. But the British were outnumbered and the French gained the advantage. Graves returned to New York to re-fit the fleet. De Grasse returned to Chesapeake Bay. By 28th September, Cornwallis was surrounded.

Cornwallis's chance of survival was slight. He wrote to Clinton: "If you cannot relieve me very soon, you must be prepared to hear the worst." He massed his forces into the strongest positions at Yorktown and the Americans and French promptly stepped into the abandoned redoubts. Siege operations began, first with entrenchments about 1,000 yards from the enemy, then with artillery bombardments to weaken the opposing lines (254). By 7th October, the first trenches were manned and

work had begun on the next line (253). On 15th October two British key redoubts, numbers nine and ten, were overrun in night attacks. Gradually the British were squeezed inward. In New York, Sir Henry Clinton collected 7,000 men to come to their rescue, but was unable to move without British ships; Graves was repairing his fleet and could not sail until 17th October. By then Cornwallis had made his last desperate throw. On 16th October men were assembled for a dash

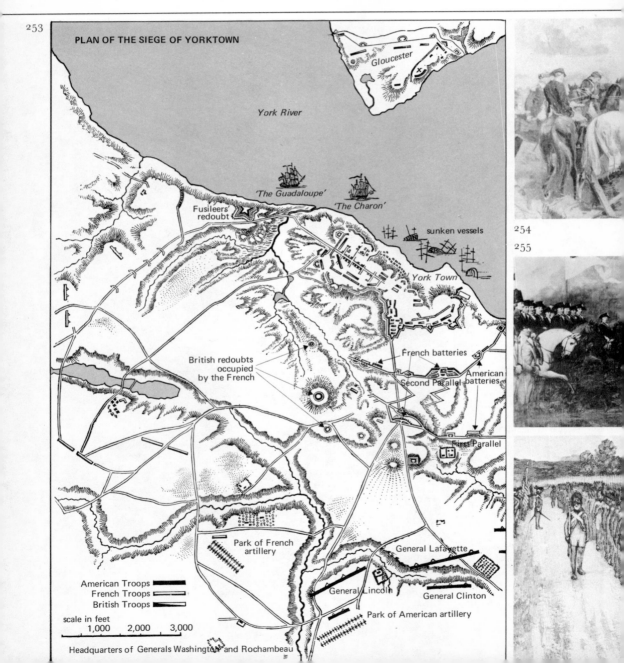

253

PLAN OF THE SIEGE OF YORKTOWN

Gloucester

York River

'The Guadaloupe'

'The Charon'

sunken vessels

254

255

Fusiliers' redoubt

York Town

British redoubts occupied by the French

French batteries

Second Parallel

American batteries

First Parallel

Park of French artillery

General Lafayette

General Clinton

American Troops

French Troops

British Troops

General Lincoln

scale in feet
1,000 2,000 3,000

Park of American artillery

Headquarters of Generals Washington and Rochambeau

across the river to slash through the enemy positions outside Gloucester on the opposite bank. But a sudden squall prevented the boats making their crossing. So, on 17th October, Cornwallis sent forward the white flag of truce and agreed to discuss terms. He could only agree to Washington's demand of complete surrender. On 19th October, 1781, at nine o'clock in the morning the terms were signed. The British main force, over 8,000 men, was to be handed over. At two o'clock that after-noon came the final humiliation, when British troops filed between the French and American forces to lay down their weapons (255, 256). Cornwallis, claiming to be ill, did not deliver his sword to Washington as custom demanded, but a junior officer did it for him. Wild American celebrations broke out, despite posted appeals for calm (257), while out past Chesapeake Bay, Clinton's overdue rescue fleet slowly tacked about on its voyage back to New York.

257

256

Illumination.

COLONEL TILGHMAN, Aid de Camp to his Excellency General WASHINGTON, having brought official acounts of the SURRENDER of Lord Cornwallis, and the Garrisons of York and Gloucester, those Citizens who chuse to ILLUMINATE on the GLORIOUS OCCASION, will do it this evening at Six, and extinguish their lights at Nine o'clock.

Decorum and harmony are earnestly recommended to every Citizen, and a general discountenance to the least appearance of riot.

October 24, 1781.

When Lord North heard of Yorktown he cried, "Oh God—it's all over!" He resigned on 20th March, 1782, and Lord Rockingham returned to power. In New York, Sir Henry Clinton was replaced by Sir Guy Carleton (259). Cornwallis, on parole, returned to explain himself and his actions in England. Although war between Britain, France and Spain continued, peace talks between Britain and America began in Paris. Little progress was made until Lord Shelbourne became prime minister following Rockingham's death on 1st July, 1782. Charles James Fox, who was in charge of European affairs, resigned, and Shelbourne (a friend of Franklin) could work more freely. Franklin (258) told Britain's envoy, that London should recognize American independence and settle generous boundaries, including the cession of Canada to America. But Shelbourne answered in August, 1782, that he would not recognize American independence until there was general peace.

258

The American negotiators, especially John Jay (260) and John Adams, became suspicious of French intentions. These fears grew when Vergennes the French minister tried to persuade them that it mattered little if Britain delayed full recognition as long as the peace was signed. Franklin and Jay were determined on complete recognition, and the British were told to bargain with "the United States of America." By 29th August, Shelbourne had reluctantly decided to ask Parliament's permission to concede American independence. In September a draft treaty was completed, though without Canada, and was formally signed on 30th November, 1782 (261). The Continental Congress ratified the treaty on 15th April, 1783, and issued a proclamation to that effect on the 17th. On the eighth anniversary of Lexington and Concord (19th April), George Washington told the news to his army. Beacon fires blazed across the country to tell of the new nation (262).

259

260

261

262

CHAPTER SEVEN

THE STRUGGLE FOR PEACE

HOW HAD THE Americans gained their victory? On the military side after Saratoga the Patriots had experienced some setbacks, but the movements forward had gradually outpaced the reverses. The Continental capital of Philadelphia was recovered, but the British had concentrated at New York and the first Franco-American operation against them was abandoned. Ill-luck continued. In the ensuing attack on Newport the storm at sea scattered the two fleets, and the action was fought between individual ships, rather than two fleets, so reducing the values of French numerical superiority.

But the British were still hard-pressed. With forces having to go to the West Indies and to the south, Clinton lacked strength enough to strike effectively from New York. In the subsequent stalemate, Clinton had been sent more troops, but these only replaced those he had sent elsewhere, and many of them contracted fever. He had asked to resign in favour of Lord Cornwallis at the end of 1779, but this request had been refused. The British conquests in the South— Savannah in 1778, Augusta in January, 1779, and Charleston in May, 1780— needed protection. So Cornwallis, who was consigned to command of the royal forces in South Carolina and Georgia by Clinton after the latter's capture of Charleston, had to fight a primarily defensive war. Such a policy could never bring victory to the British. The longer

the war, the harder it would be to crush the Patriots. Nor could the whole of the South be held down by force: there were not enough men. And in their victories often more British than American soldiers were lost; after Cowpens, Charles James Fox commented, "Another such victory would ruin the British Army." So the British had to pull back to the coast and to Charleston. Territorial gains could not be consolidated and the British successes could only be temporary while there were too few forces to back them up. Charleston in turn had to be evacuated and Cornwallis had to move northward to counter the threat in Virginia, later to be tied down, surrounded and defeated at Yorktown. Lack of troops, and British vulnerability at New York, deprived him of timely aid; the French threat in the West Indies meant insufficient Royal Navy ships were sent to remove the French fleet closing his sea escape route.

The tide ran against the British, even without the mistakes of their commanders. The war was one of attrition, and the Americans had the advantage. Their strength lay in the ideological factor. The army was based on soldiers volunteering to fight, returning to their peacetime occupations, then returning to fight again. There was a close unity between army and people: both were struggling for an idea, and an ideal—freedom. They were demanding what they regarded as their right. They sought not to conquer territories, nor even to defeat the opposing army. Nor did they need to do this; all they had to do was to convince the opposing side it was wasteful and useless to continue. Such a war, if supported by sufficient people with sufficient conviction, is difficult to lose. Provided the Patriots could ride the storm, keep coming back, all the time using the Declaration of Independence as their banner, the British had an almost impossible task. They had to suffocate an entire country, and this they could never do. The Americans bent a little under the strain, as when the Pennsylvania Line mutinied, but the British bent farther and broke. And even if the Americans had been defeated, the idea would have lived on for another time.

But America still had to win the peace, and here few countries felt she could succeed. It was strongly doubted that the new republic would survive. Franklin, in Paris, alone declared that America would survive and prosper. The Anglo-American treaty did not take full effect until the autumn of 1783. Preliminary agreements were also made between Britain, France and Spain in January, 1783, with the final peace signed in Paris on 3rd September. America benefited most in territorial terms. Spain obtained Minorca and the Floridas, although not Gibraltar. France gained little except the satisfaction of seeing Britain defeated. The crippling cost of the war brought her nearer to bankruptcy and the start of the French Revolution six years later. Neither France, nor Spain, could now be relied upon as allies for America. Both had helped the Patriots during the war mainly for their own ends. Spain had not even recognized American independence, and had suspected American intentions toward Spanish possessions in North America. In 1780 John Jay had been sent to Madrid to try and improve relations, but with little success. Most European courts now predicted that America would collapse, leaving them to take the pickings. With difficulty the country had unified itself for the war, and managed to maintain and strengthen that unity during the war years. But war produces a common cause: peace does not give such an obvious bond.

In 1783 the third and perhaps most critical phase of America's struggle began. The immediate after effects of war had to be solved. Then a sound system of government had to be established—and there were still conflicting views about this. Momentous events would soon occur in Europe. The French Revolution would inflame all nations, and aggravate the conflict between Federalists and Republicans. But thanks to George Washington's neutralism and isolationism America was to be left alone: European states were busy with their own affairs. So America was able to emerge healthy from the vulnerable years of adolescence. Party politics were to rise and the single father-figure of George Washington was to slip away. Democracy was to come, with all its ideals and betrayals, its hopes and its disappointments. America would then be growing up.

Carleton evacuated New York in November, 1783, and with the abandonment of posts on the Penobscot River in Maine in January, 1784, the last British troops left America (263, 264); Washington had already triumphantly entered New York in November (265). But the people, though freed from the strain of war, still had to suffer the pangs of peace. In the economic depression of 1785 and 1786, farmers and merchants lost a profitable market; markets in Britain and elsewhere in the Empire disappeared, and new markets had not yet been found. American maritime trade only regained its pre-war level in 1788. British creditors claimed their money, currency was short, and many states raised taxes. Inevitably, the situation sometimes became violent. In Massachusetts an open revolt took place in late 1786 when farmers rose to defend their homes against creditors, the state legislature having refused to offer them relief. The insurrection was soon put down in eastern

263

265

264

Massachusetts, but continued longer in the western half of the state under the leadership of a Patriot officer, Daniel Shays (266). On 26th January, 1787, Shays and 1,200 followers attacked, though unsuccessfully, the state arsenal at Springfield. There was also violence against the Loyalists who had supported Britain during the war, and John Adams claimed that one-third of the Americans were Loyalists at heart. They were more numerous in New York and in the South. From 1777 onward, the states had banished prominent Loyalists, and others ran the risk of being tarred and feathered or worse (267). By the end of the war up to 80,000 Americans had been banished or had emigrated. The peace treaty itself called upon Congress to "earnestly recommend" that state laws against Loyalists should be scrapped. Some states did so quickly, but in a few cases penalties were imposed for over ten years.

266

267

Articles of Confederation were signed between the states in 1777, but these only established a "superintending power." A permanent governmental system needed to be formed. Through the efforts of Alexander Hamilton (268) and James Madison (269) the Federal Convention met in May, 1797. The Virginians demanded a two-chamber Congress, with the lower house elected by the people and the upper by the lower. To counter this William Paterson suggested the "New Jersey Plan" with one house elected by the states, regardless of their populations. This was criticized for giving the states too much power. Then the "Connecticut Compromise" was agreed: the House of Representatives should draw its members from districts according to their population, and the Senate two delegates from each state, regardless of their populations. But quarrels continued, especially about the right of slaves to vote, and also about external taxation and commerce. Again a compromise

268   269

271

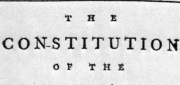

THE
CONSTITUTION
OF THE
United States of America.

Frame of Government.

WE, the People of the UNITED STATES, in order to form a more perfect union, establish justice, insure domestic tranquility, provide for the common defence, promote the general welfare, and secure the blessings of liberty to ourselves and our posterity, do ordain and establish this Constitution for the United States of AMERICA.

270

272

273

was reached. Congress would impose import but not export duties, and a slave would count as three-fifths of a person for voting and taxation. In autumn, 1787, the "Fifty-five Founding Fathers" finished drafting the Constitution (270, 271) which then went to the states for signature and discussion. To encourage agreement, Hamilton, Madison and Jay wrote *The Federalist*, a series of essays arguing that the Constitution made a true balance between the central government and the states. But Anti-

Federalists, including Patrick Henry, Richard Henry Lee and George Clinton, declared that the Articles of Confederation should remain a "superintending power." Liberals wanted a Bill of Rights to protect individual liberties, which was added in 1791. Gradually, the Constitution was endorsed and in June, 1788, it was ratified. Celebrations were held (272), and the Senate and House of Representatives began to meet at Constitution Hall, Philadelphia (273, 274).

With the Constitution ratified, Washington was widely expected to be the first President (276). Indeed, in the closing months of the war there had even been a move to persuade him to accept an American Crown. Astonished, Washington at once rejected the idea: "Let me beseech you . . . if you have any regard for your country, concern for yourself or posterity, or respect for me, to banish these thoughts from your mind." Nevertheless, Washington was treated almost like royalty. On 4th December, 1783, he made a ceremonial journey to hand over his commission to Congress. He would take "leave of all the employments of public life." He returned to his beautiful mansion at Mount Vernon as a civilian (275). But the house remained a focal point, as it had during the war, where Washington received important visitors like Lafayette (279). On the first Wednesday in February, 1789, in the first presidential election, Washington was unanimously chosen, with John Adams as his

Vice-President. Again Washington was treated like a king; as he sailed to New York a ship's choir even sang his praises to the tune of *God Save the King*. Crowds celebrated everywhere (277). After his inauguration on 30th April in New York (278) Washington showed, as he had often done before, that he was no democrat. He believed in strong central government and a strong President. He was against party politics. Working with a small staff of unpaid clerks, Washington faced many problems. Paper money was still worthless, and hard currency short; only three banks functioned (280). The American Army totalled only 840 officers and men. North Carolina and Rhode Island were still outside the Union; Britain clung to her western posts and was suspected of intriguing with the Indians. Washington appointed Thomas Jefferson Secretary of State, and Alexander Hamilton Secretary of the Treasury. There was to be increasing conflict between the two.

276

277

278

279

280

Even before the states had signed the Articles of Confederation in 1777, the South-North conflict had begun. Men from Maryland, Virginia, the Carolinas, and Georgia objected to being ruled from Philadelphia, and the terms "Southern States" and "Northern States" were becoming current. Northern and southern attitudes polarized on the issue of slavery. Many in the South tried to portray the system as happy and beneficial to the Negroes (281), but inevitably the North remained more anti-slavery than the South. It became clear that the Mason-Dixon Line divided one region from the other. A vast difference characterized ordinary life in the South (282) and that in the North (283). Quarrelling continued during peacetime. Congress, said the South, should exert pressure upon Spain to open the Mississippi to the largest American ships. Already the higher reaches were used as a main means of transportation (284); but the North was

281

more reluctant. In discussions about the site of the national capital, complete separation each side of the Mason-Dixon line was debated. Various states disputed over claims for the vast areas of new land opened up by the British defeat. This age of "Westward Ho!" was illustrated a few years later by the painter Emanuel Gottlieb Leutze (285). In 1785 and 1787 Congress drew up two ordinances for the Northwest, and out of this region the states of Ohio, Indiana, Illinois, Michigan and Wisconsin were to be formed. In the Old Southwest in 1776, Virginia took territory under its protection called Kentucky. Vermont became a state in 1791 and Kentucky one in 1792. Tennessee, formed by a merger of the Watauga and Cumberland settlements, became a state in 1796. But claims and counter-claims continued. Indian clashes constantly troubled the national government; and frontier life was still as hard as ever (286).

284

283

285

286

President Washington continued to think like a military man. He disliked committees and relied more and more upon his small Cabinet: Jefferson, Hamilton, and Henry Knox, the Secretary of War (287). But Hamilton and Jefferson increasingly drew apart. Hamilton was the exponent of High Federalism, of strong authority vested in the central government (289). Jefferson's views were often directly opposed. Jefferson welcomed Tom Paine's *Rights of Man*, dedicated to Washington. A bitter press campaign broke out, centring upon Federalism versus state rights. Washington wished to retire at the end of his first Presidential term in 1792, but was persuaded to stay on. Jefferson said: "North and South will hang together if they have you to hang on to." So, on 4th March, 1793, Washington was re-inaugurated. In the same year war broke out in Europe, as the French Revolutionaries had executed their King, Louis XVI, and threatened to destroy Euro-

288

287

289

pean monarchy as a whole. Washington wanted neutrality and was supported by Hamilton. But Jefferson believed that America owed obligations to the French people, and to the cause of universal liberty. The Democratic Societies, or Jacobin Clubs, became part of a party led by Jefferson, with his home at Monticello as its base (288, 291). Washington, however, with Hamilton, continually stressed neutrality and the need for strong central government. Washington's authoritarianism was shown when, during the 1794 rebellion in Pennsylvania against the excise tax, and against the wishes of Jeffersonians, he called out the militia (290). Also against Jefferson's wishes, Washington concluded a treaty with the British in April, 1794. Washington welcomed the end of his second Presidential term. In September, 1796, Washington gave his Farewell Address, and retired. The United States of America, young, vigorous, and above all independent, was left to develop alone.

FURTHER READING

J. R. Alden, *History of the American Revolution* (New York, 1969 and London, 1969)

    The American Revolution 1775–1783 (New York, 1954 and London, 1954)

    John Stuart and the Southern Colonial Frontier, 1754–1775 (Ann Arbor, Michigan, 1944 and London, 1944)

    The First South (Baton Rouge, 1961)

Charles M. Andrews, *The Colonial Background of the American Revolution* (New Haven, 1924 and London, 1924)

Bernard Bailyn, *The Ideological Origins of the American Revolution* (Cambridge, Mass., 1967)

J. Bakeless, *Background to Glory: The Life of George Rogers Clark* (Philadelphia, 1957)

Samuel Bemis, *Diplomacy of the American Revolution* (New York, 1935 and London, 1935)

G. A. Billias, *George Washington's Generals* (New York, 1964)

J. Brooke, *The Chatham Administration 1766–68* (New York, 1956 and London, 1950)

E. Burnett, *The Continental Congress* (New York, 1941)

I. R. Christie, *The End of North's Ministry 1780–1782* (New York, 1958 and London, 1958)

Verner Crane, *Benjamin Franklin, Englishman and American* (Baltimore, 1936)

M. Farrand, *The Framing of the Constitution of the United States* (New Haven, 1913 and London, 1913)

D. S. Freeman, *George Washington: A Biography* (New York, 1948–57 and London, 1948)

L. Gottschalk, *Lafayette and the Close of the American Revolution* (Chicago, 1942 and London, 1942)

L. Hartz, *The Liberal Tradition in America* (New York, 1955)

B. Knollenberg, *Origin of the American Revolution 1759–66* (New York, 1960 and London, 1959)

D. Lacy, *The Meaning of the American Revolution* (New York, 1964 and London, 1967)

D. Malone, *Jefferson* (Boston, 1948 and London, 1949)

J. C. Miller, *Origins of the American Revolution* (Boston, 1943 and London, 1960)

    Triumph of Freedom 1775–1783 (Boston, 1948)

L. B. Namier and J. Brooke, *The History of Parliament: The House of Commons 1754–1790* (New York, 1964 and London, 1964)

    Charles Townshend (New York, 1964 and London, 1964)

R. R. Palmer, *The Age of the Democratic Revolution: A Political History of Europe and America 1760–1800* (Princeton, 1959–64 and London, 1960)

H. H. Peckham, *The War of Independence* (Chicago, 1958 and London, 1958)

Hugh Rankin, ed., *The American Revolution* (New York, 1965 and London, 1964)

C. R. Ritcheson, *British Politics and the American Revolution* (Norman, Oklahoma, 1954)

PICTURE CREDITS

INDEX